*A nicely illustrated and inherently fascinating read throughout,* Nine Perfect Petals: The Enneagram for Flower Gardeners *is an especially and unreservedly recommended addition to personal, professional, and community library Flower Gardening, Popular Psychology, and Personal Self-Help/Self-Improvement collections. It should be noted that* Nine Perfect Petals *is readily available in hardback, paperback, and ebook editions.* – **James A. Cox,** Editor-in-Chief, *Midwest Book Review*

*With wit and solid horticultural knowledge, Dr. Rosenberg delivers a charming, informative, and beautifully illustrated exposition of the Enneagram, the most rational and useful of all self-improvement regimes.* – **Dan Lewandowski,** author of *Worth Winning*

*Once you know the Enneagram, you see it in everything. Dr. Angela Rosenberg finds it in the garden and in relationships. Flower beds are fertile ground for exploring the many dimensions and nuances of the Enneagram. The author's passion for both gardening and the Enneagram pour out of the pages, making for a delightful and impactful read.* – **Matt Schlegel,** author of *Teamwork 9.0—Successful Workgroup Problem Solving Using the Enneagram*

*Full of wisdom and with an absolutely authentic voice, this book is an insightful work for the green or brown thumb alike. As a non-gardener, I gained illumination about what "makes people tick" and found some inspiration to try my Type 3 hand out at tilling a row or two!* – **Claudia S. P. Fernandez, DrPH, MS, RD, LDN,** author of *It-Factor Leadership: Become a Better Leader in 13 Steps*

*Type manifests in every facet of life. The author looks at Enneagram types through the interactions of the gardener and her garden. If you garden (or love those who do), you will see people you know in the pages of this book. Rosenberg achieves a beautiful integration of a deep knowledge of flowers, essences, art, poetry, symbology, and history with an equally deep understanding of the Enneagram. She includes carefully chosen quotes that hit the spot for each type. Her writing style is light, with moments of lyrical delight that will bring a smile to your face. I'm not a pun guy, but I chuckled at lots of her garden puns. Her style is whimsical, but also gentle, nurturing, and inspiring. This book will introduce the Enneagram to a whole new crop of people who will fall in love with the system.* – **Roger Hall, PhD,** Compass Consultation, Ltd., author of *Staying Happy Being Productive*

*This book is a wonderful way for flower lovers, gardeners, skeptics, and nature lovers to find their way to the Enneagram. They will totally enjoy reading and growing in natural time with* Nine Perfect Petals. *The author's humor, wordplay, and knowledge of the Enneagram naturally flow in a fun, magical, diverse garden of a book.* – **Kate Finlayson,** *Creator of Dancing the Enneagram*

Nine Perfect Petals *by Angela M Rosenberg is a painstakingly curated and colorfully illustrated guide to the Enneagram for flower gardeners. By relating to how a person maintains their garden, Dr. Rosenberg explains the Enneagram personality typology. . . . This book also includes characteristics, strengths, weaknesses, and pathways for individual growth and well-being, customized to one's personality type. Should you need another reason to pick up this book, thought-provoking quotes are included regularly in the book.*

*With brilliant watercolor illustrations and eye-catching headings, this book had me hooked from the first page. The author's unique voice shines in her clear explanations and whimsical allusions to gardening practices. I found it easy to spot my core persona, and I loved how she took it a step further and gave helpful tips for self-growth. By the author providing several tables in the last few pages, I found it easier to absorb the information. Dr. Rosenberg's analogies to several flowers, including roses, have forever changed how I perceive them, and I will always connect them to the Enneagram. Overall, this book is a must-read and appeals to all, even those who are not avid gardeners.* – **Cassie Widjaja** for *Readers' Favorite*

*Learning about ourselves is a constant journey that can be rewarding and challenging, depending upon where we are within the fork in the road. You can learn more about yourself and gardening characteristics in the book,* Nine Perfect Petals: The Enneagram for Flower Gardeners. *This book offers a wonderful viewpoint that . . . thoroughly explains how all of these [Enneagram] pieces work together by introducing the reader to the various flowers associated with the Enneagram: Head=Thinking (Zinnia, Hollyhock, and Orchid), Heart=Feeling (Bloodroot, Lavender, and Clematis), and Gut=Instinct (Rose, Windflower, and Black-Eyed Susan), [as well as] the relationships and connection between the gardener and their garden, the strengths and challenges in cultivating the garden, and tips for the gardener to aid in creating a more cohesive gardening experience.*

*I enjoyed this book because it has a coffee-table-book appeal due to its illuminating visual presence. Throughout the book . . . there are illustrations of beautiful flowers by Hui Jing Ng (which were breathtaking), quotes by various authors, and a colorful allure that creates an aesthetic flair for the reader.* Nine Perfect Petals *offers a calming presence which means that if you're not currently interested in gardening, you will be within the first ten pages. . . . Find your peace, pathway, purpose, and passion through* Nine Perfect Petals. *Strongly recommended.* – **Vernita Naylor** for *Readers' Favorite*

*This delightful book is dedicated to discovering the Enneagram personality types in correlation with flower gardening. . . .* Nine Perfect Petals *is the ideal companion to find out which of the nine personality types suits you best. . . . I did not expect that a book on the Enneagram could be enlightening and fun at the same time, but it is a good writer's job to surprise their readers, and Rosenberg impressed me a great deal. Although I am not a flower gardener,* Nine Perfect Petals *allowed me to learn about a subject I have wanted to explore for a long time. . . . I was also fascinated by the many beautiful and colorful images. . . . I recommend* Nine Perfect Petals *to anyone who wants to know more about the Enneagram and who is looking for a pleasant and enlightening explanation. Rosenberg will not let her readers down.* – **Astrid Iustulin** for *Readers' Favorite*

# Nine Perfect Petals

## The Enneagram for Flower Gardeners

ANGELA MCCAFFREY ROSENBERG

BOOK ONE IN THE ENNEAGRAM IN NATURE SERIES

ISBN: 978-1-7366767-0-7 (hard cover)
ISBN: 978-1-7366767-1-4 (ebook)
ISBN: 978-1-7366767-2-1 (paperback)

Library of Congress Control Number: 2021904896

Cover design: Ng Hui Jing

All illustrations: Ng Hui Jing

Interior design: MediaNeighbours.com

*To my husband, Marty, who continues
to encourage me to grow.*

# Contents

Preface: The Nine Enneagram Types in the Garden .................................... ix

Introduction Part 1: What Is Your Hue? ...................................................... xv
    The Enneagram Typology ............................................................................ xv

Introduction Part 2: Enneagram Triads, Wings, Arrows, and Essences .... xxiii
    The Enneagram Triads ................................................................................ xxiv
        Feeling (2-3-4s) .................................................................................... xxv
        Thinking (5-6-7s) ................................................................................. xxv
        Instinct (8-9-1s) .................................................................................. xxvi
    Arrows (Paths) and Wings ......................................................................... xxvii
        Follow the Arrows (Paths) ................................................................... xxvii
        Lean on Your Wings ............................................................................. xxx
    Changing the Hue of You ............................................................................ xxx
    In Essence ................................................................................................... xxxi

Enneagram Type Chapters, 1 through 9
    1. The Perfect Gardener – Rose ..................................................................... 1
    2. The Helpful Gardener – Zinnia ................................................................ 13
    3. The Efficient Gardener – Hollyhock ....................................................... 25
    4. The Aesthetic Gardener – Orchid ............................................................ 37
    5. The Observant Gardener – Bloodroot ..................................................... 49
    6. The Cautious Gardener – Lavender .......................................................... 61
    7. The Adventurous Gardener – Clematis .................................................... 73
    8. The Self-reliant Gardener – Black-eyed Susan ........................................ 85
    9. The Peaceful Gardener – Windflower ...................................................... 97

Appendices
    Table 1: Passions of the Enneagram Type ................................................... 110
    Table 2: Passions, Tools, and Symbols by Type .......................................... 111
    Table 3: Flower, Scientific Name, Reason, Preference ................................. 114

Acknowledgments .......................................................................................... 119

About the Author ........................................................................................... 121

**Additionally, the 9 Flower Gardener chapters discuss the following:**

The Enneagram Gardener Type Checklist
The Blossoms: The Strengths of the Gardener Type
The Weeds: The Challenges for the Gardener Type
Knowing When the Type Is in the Brambles (Turn Back!)
How to Find Your Path "Home"
The Meaning of the Type Flower
Essences and Flower Alternatives
Distinctive Hues of the Flower Gardener Type
Tips for Type

SHOW ME YOUR GARDEN
AND I WILL TELL YOU WHAT YOU ARE.

ALFRED AUSTIN

I AM A flower gardener. And my story opens twenty-five years ago when I made the journey to begin my new life at an eighty-year-old farmhouse on seventy-five acres of land, in Pittsboro, North Carolina. This adventure started in 1996 when I married a vegetable gardener and love of my life, Marty. Coincidentally, shortly before my move to North Carolina, my sister JoAnn had introduced me to the Enneagram during an intense period of loss and personal growth for both of us. Little did I know, as is true for many of life's loves and passions, the garden and Enneagram paths would eventually cross.

The Enneagram is a nine-pointed circular figure that is used to display nine distinctly different, yet connected, personality *types* or *points*. This array of types is often compared to a spectrum of colors, with each of us comprising all hues, but only one hue/type characterizing an individual. According to Enneagram theory, each of these types is a manifestation of one of the essential characteristics of the divine (however that is understood by you); and together, they represent the complete unity and fullness of humankind.

So, what does the Enneagram have to do with gardening? I begin with a quote widely attributed to George Bernard Shaw: *The best place to find God is in a garden. You can dig for him there.* As a gardener, this quote always resonated with me. I suspect many would say they look to the heavens to find God. I suppose I would say that I find God in the dirt. The serenity of gently placing a seed in the soil, of the tender shoots of early spring blossoms, and of mulching perennials for their winter's rest have taught me to be still—and find the divine in the natural world. Over the last twenty-five years, as I continued to expand the colors and varieties of plants in my garden, I began to note the similarities between gardening and the *Enneagram*.

I recall one of the first times I awakened to the notion of the relationship between the Enneagram types and flower gardening. A dear friend had bought a nearby farm and was beginning her gardening journey in earnest. Having visited my garden, she asked what books I might recommend to get her started. Dumbfounded, I realized that I wasn't able to share a single recommendation. Not one. Upon introspection, I realized that I had been so busy hauling rocks, digging through clay, and pulling out invasive English ivy that I hadn't read or studied any books related to gardening in the North Carolina heat and red-clay soil. That was my *aha* moment. I began to observe my fellow flower gardeners' Enneagram types and how their unique personality characteristics were manifested in their relationship with nature and their gardening habits and rituals. As a professional leadership trainer and coach, I was motivated to discover what I could determine about personality types by observing gardeners and their garden practices.

So, you might conclude, a personality typology used and believed by hordes of people, including myself, must be scientifically valid! Nope. Absolutely no scientific evidence! However, after thirty years of using this typology in my work, I have one response to the naysayers: in terms of a typology for explaining human motivation and experience, it is *spot on*. However, if you are seeking a deep psychological dive into the Enneagram, this is perhaps not the book for you. There are tomes of complex scholarly works on this ancient system of personality typing, with applications running the gamut from the spiritual to the business environment. The authors of these works have analyzed the Enneagram in great depth, and I admire their insights and direction, as their work has undoubtedly altered my self-understanding and my ongoing quest to better understand and relate to others. I would wholeheartedly advise you to consult one or more of the complex scholarly works on this ancient system of personality typing to learn about its application to your specific journey. However, if you care to dig deep, garden-style, join me in reading this whimsical, informative, Enneagram book. The following chapters will detail nine distinct flower gardens to facilitate your comprehension of the nine types, as well as specific garden paths to move each type to a more secure and resourceful state through an appreciation of the Enneagram arrows.

So, it is within my garden, under the shade of a wide-brimmed hat, that I have come to more deeply know others and my own particular type. Over the course of reading this book, I hope that you, too, will come to deepen your awareness of the Enneagram and how it is manifested through your own and your friends' flower gardens.

*Without courage,*
*wisdom bears no fruit.*
Baltasar Gracián

Nature has an uncanny way of connecting us as much as it differentiates us. Whether in a flower garden, up in the air, or on the floor of the ocean, we come to connect with natural wonders and also witness the different colors, species, and functions that the natural world has to teach us. In these times, we begin to discern our great and small contributions to the universe—to life. Similarly, the Enneagram typology connects and differentiates us as fellow humans. In the following nine chapters, you will come to know and appreciate the Nine Enneagram Types through the lens of the flower garden—Nine Perfect Petals. We will examine type characteristics, strengths, and challenges through identifying garden flowers and practices. We will also explore flower meanings and essences as one flower-power mechanism to strive for well-being.

The Introduction: Part 1 will provide a brief description of the Enneagram and *Descriptions of the Nine Types in the Garden*. The Introduction: Part 2 provides an overview of the Enneagram *Triads, Wings, Arrows,* and *Essences*. The following nine chapters will focus on the *Nine Perfect Petals;* i.e., the nine Enneagram personality types in the context of the flower garden. Each chapter contains the following sections:

- Type Description and Flower

- The Enneagram Gardener Type Checklist

- The Blossoms/Strengths of the Enneagram Type

- The Weeds/Challenges of the Enneagram Type

- In the Brambles

- The Path Home

- In Essence

- Key Type Attributes ("Distinctive Hues")
- Tips for Type

Moreover, in the Appendices, a number of tables will provide:

- An overview of gardener types, passions, and tools;
- A full description of the nine passions; and
- Scientific names of flowers, why they are assigned to a type, and their sun/shade preference

I hope that as you read about each of the *Nine Perfect Petals*, with their abundant blossoms and burdensome weeds, you will come to discover the divine in nature, your fellow gardeners, and most importantly, yourself.

We're all just walking each other home.

Ram Dass

# Introduction Part 1:
## What Is Your Hue?
## The Nine Enneagram Types
## in the Garden

### The Enneagram Typology

The Enneagram (Greek term, meaning *nine points*) is a personality typology that describes nine distinct (personality) points, each reflecting a core, divine quality. The Enneagram has deep roots and many branches. Some Enneagram scholars suggest the diagram was inscribed in ancient texts by Sufi tribes seeking to find the truth of divine love and knowledge through a direct, personal experience of God; others believe it originated in the Middle Ages. Regardless, the typology and the descriptions of the nine personality types, with their associated characteristics, have been well recognized throughout the centuries and among various countries and cultures, with applications across professional disciplines.

The Enneagram diagram is a nine-pointed figure that has often been compared to a color wheel or prism, which upon exposure to white light, fans into a spectrum of basic colors. With this metaphor, every person contains all of the hues, but one particular color stands out—the specific hue of that individual. This hue equates to one of the nine Enneagram types and all of the associated characteristics of that type.

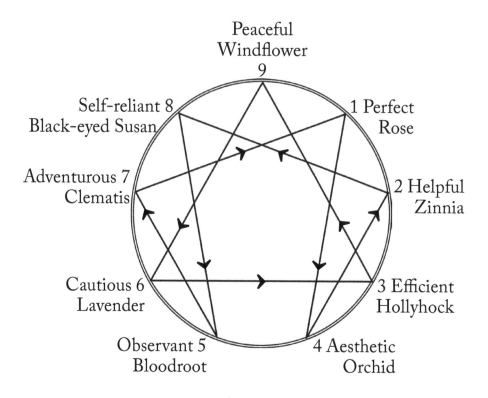

Choosing a specific flower for each Enneagram point is akin to choosing one's favorite child or grandchild—an impossible endeavor. So, what method could I follow to make such an unfeasible decision and apply that to this much-lauded and complex personality typology?

In truth, I turned to the Enneagram Triads (see page xxiv) to guide my decision. I first looked to the Thinking (Head) Triad to study flower meanings from a variety of different sources. From that search I derived a list of flowers that represented the particular qualities, attributes, and characteristics of each Enneagram point. For example, the hollyhock flower aptly mirrors the Type 3's distinguishing trait of ambition.

Essentially, I imagined a particular Type as a flower, and it made sense! Next I moved on to the Feeling (Heart) Triad to winnow my list to those flowers that looked, felt, and behaved like the Type. At this juncture, and with at times a myriad of flower choices remaining for each point, I turned to the Instinctual (Gut) Triad and went with my intuition to choose a flower for each of the nine points.

As I made my final flower designations, I became convinced that the Enneagram can be applied to the natural world as well as to people. From there, I excitedly turned to contemplation of Flower Gardener Types. With twenty-five years of exploring the Enneagram as a professional leadership trainer and coach, I can now present to you the 9 points of the Enneagram Typology as *Nine Perfect Petals*.

## TYPE 1: THE PERFECT GARDENER
### ROSE

The flower garden of the Type 1 will be designed with an eye toward perfection. In life and in the garden, the 1 Flower Gardener thoughtfully plans every aspect of her flower garden to meet her own and garden visitors' highest standards. She very deliberately conceives her garden to include native plants, solar lighting, and drip irrigation, with a lens toward conserving increasingly scarce natural resources. Her flower garden is a "righteous" garden and will meet the gold standard for environmentally conscious garden practices. If there was a gardener prize titled "Gardener for the Greater Good," it would be an apt award for the 1 Flower Gardener.

## TYPE 2: THE HELPFUL GARDENER
### ZINNIA

The flower garden of the Type 2 is rife with flowers and plants that are meant for showing and sharing. The 2 Flower Gardener is an appreciative, giving person, and intentionally chooses plants that will appeal to friends, family, and garden visitors and is always willing to share cuttings and vases of blooms. Open to color and texture, the Type 2 in life and garden gets great joy from designing, picking, and donating her flowers through charity events and weddings. If there is such a title as the "The Giving Gardener"—it would surely describe the Type 2.

## TYPE 3: THE EFFICIENT GARDENER
## HOLLYHOCK

The flower garden of the Type 3 is more than likely *multiple* flower gardens. The efficient and ambitious 3 Flower Gardener is bound and determined to create a variety of gardens, each with a distinct meaning and purpose. The Three in life and garden embraces the concept of show and tell. She will host morning tea in her shade garden and cut copious sun-garden blooms after noon to sell at the local farmers' market. The efficient 3 Flower Gardener is all about making the most of her garden by creating practical, useful design features. If you are in search of a "Resourceful Gardener," look no further than a Type 3.

## Type 4: The Aesthetic Gardener
### Orchid

The flower garden of the Type 4 is a sanctuary of discovery and rare beauty. Whatever the "special feature"—there will be one or more beds with distinctive visual appeal—characterizing the aesthetic qualities of the Four. The 4 Flower Gardener will invite you as a special guest to embrace a path laden with Jack in the Pulpits or their rare orchid house. Wherever it may be, the Type 4 sanctuary will be a "Garden of Unique Appeal," and if you have the good fortune of befriending a Type 4—you will find quality garden time reserved just for you.

## Type 5: The Observant Gardener
### Bloodroot

The garden of the Type 5, on approach, will seem to be nothing at all—until you peer beyond the entrance gate. For the 5 Flower Gardener, in life and garden, in the mind is where their wisdom and depth is carefully protected. The Type 5 wisely reflects and designs her garden with self-sufficient plants, as her garden is less about work and more about peaceful meditation and sanctuary. A blooming succulent garden would be fitting for a Five, given their intrinsic irrigation system! And cacti have a way of discouraging a lot of touchy-feely garden dwellers! If you are looking for a "Perceptive Gardener," enjoy the company of the discerning Type 5.

## Type 6: The Cautious Gardener
### Lavender

The garden of the Type 6 will be meticulously researched and planned because the Six in life and garden is prepared! The 6 Flower Gardener will have consulted with a variety of flower garden specialists and, when feeling confident, will forge ahead! The soil will be amended and the irrigation systems thoughtfully planned to withstand drought conditions. Fencing for deer will be an absolute, with plants chosen to meet the correct Zone conditions. The garden of the Type 6 is definitely "Well Equipped" for the next garden apocalypse—so if you need shelter for your flowers in a storm, find a Type 6 Flower Gardener!

## Type 7: The Adventurous Gardener
### Clematis

The garden of the Type 7 is chock full of imagination and fun, as these are the gifts of the 7 Flower Gardener! This garden is a space where ideas and possibilities are not only sowed but are nurtured and thrive! You will often find many species of plants and perhaps creative ecosystems, depending upon the ingenuity and budget of the gardener. Waterfalls, peacocks, koi, pergolas . . . and did I see a monkey? A "Joy-full" garden is this one, so consider yourself in Garden-Disney for the day. Enjoy the wild ride!

## Type 8: The Self-reliant Gardener
### Black-eyed Susan

The garden of the Type 8 will be robust and lush in a rock wall, with a row of big, flowering shrubs—as 8 Flower Gardeners go Big or get out of the garden! Type 8s also tend to create gardens that are hearty, practical, and self-sustaining. Oh, please—they have no need for a high-maintenance garden! However, Eights in life and garden do lust for intensity, so this garden will have robust colors, strong scents,  and noticeable blooms. No Snowdrops for the 8 Flower Gardener—her garden will be bold and expressive. And once an 8 is in the garden, she is all in—no half-way garden here. If you want to experience "Big Bloomers"—find yourself in the garden of an Eight.

## Type 9: The Peaceful Gardener
### Windflower

The garden of the Type 9 progresses at an unhurried pace—as Nines are all about keeping life peaceful. Perhaps you will find this garden unfinished, *a work in progress*, as is the 9 Flower Gardener—always striving to find her way, find herself, by merging with the interests (and perhaps the gardens) of others. There is no sense of worry or scurry in this garden, with the exception of the squirrel population. In the Type 9 garden, there is room for  welcome distractions that relieve the tedium of weeding and potting. This is truly a garden representing "Peace on Earth."

GARDENS ARE NOT MADE BY SINGING,
"OH, HOW BEAUTIFUL,"
AND SITTING IN THE SHADE.

RUDYARD KIPLING

# Introduction Part 2: Enneagram Triads, Wings, Arrows, and Essences

HAVE YOU EVER heard, "Some people are sleepwalking through life"? The Enneagram typology would support this concept, and perhaps take it a step further, suggesting that all of us live in a bit of a trance. We move through our daily interactions responding to people and events in somewhat predictable, patterned, and often compulsive ways. According to the Enneagram, these patterns began when we were very young, in response to a world that became increasingly complex and unpredictable.

But the Enneagram aids us by making a very important distinction between the core *essence* of who we are and the *personality* characteristics we routinely display. Our divine core essence (core Enneagram type) is the real deal, the self we touch upon when we dig deep into our core being.

However, to cope with all of the ups and downs in life that create feelings of security and stress, we begin to favor some of these core values and abilities more than others. In this way, we begin to prefer characteristic ways of *perceiving, feeling, and doing*. These adaptations help us to cope and protect our vulnerable core essence; however, in the process of donning our *personality characteristics*, we shed and bury our beautiful core essence. The good news is that, through an understanding of the Enneagram *Triads, Wings,* and *Arrows,* we can gain insight into the paths of resilience and re-connection with our divine core qualities.

> *A flower's appeal is in its contradictions—so delicate in form*
> *yet strong in fragrance, so small in size yet big in beauty, so*
> *short in life yet long on effect.*
> Terri Guillemets

## THE ENNEAGRAM TRIADS

Not unlike how the seasons of the year guide and inform our gardening practices and rituals, the Triads are a natural place to begin our garden journey to probe the Enneagram. Referred to by some as the three *centers of energy,* the triads are, in my humble opinion, the best way to gain familiarity with the motivations that are the core of the Enneagram personality typology. Each of the three triads contains three of the nine Enneagram types. The first I will describe includes types Two, Three, and Four (2-3-4s). The second triad includes types Five, Six, and Seven (5-6-7s). The third triad includes types Eight, Nine, and One (8-9-1s). Various authors use key descriptors to describe each of the Triads, but for the purpose of this book, I will use the terms I feel are most relevant to the garden:

- *Feeling* (heart) for 2-3-4s
- *Thinking* (head) for 5-6-7s
- *Instinct* (gut) for 8-9-1s

You have surely heard the old adage, "You can't judge a book by its cover." Likewise, one shouldn't judge human personality based on behavior! Rather, we must dig deep to explore our own motivations and perhaps gain insight into the motivations that inspire and challenge the behavior of others. That said, join me in exploring the Triads—three distinct approaches to life, perhaps the seasons of our personality.

## FEELING (2-3-4s)

Also known as the *heart* triad, individuals who reside in this group appear the most emotional of all types, while in fact, may be least in touch with their true emotions. The concept of *feeling* for this gardener is their focus on their own value. Those residing in this triad are concerned with their own image and how they are viewed by others. Shame is a common emotion for gar-

deners in this triad, and they exercise their right to exist without having to prove their worth. As a result of this need, gardeners in this triad will keep *doing*, embarking on the next task to validate their worth in the garden. At some level, 2-3-4s are all acting a part, and are skilled at performing the role that is needed for the situation. Those in this triad are often described as *moving outward*, in that they display a need to relate and engage with others in order to relate to life. As gardeners, 2-3-4s will generally engage through their feelings in some way or another. A 2 Flower Gardener will focus on sharing and helping others, forgetting her own garden needs a gloved hand. The 3 Flower Gardener has trouble relating to her own/others feelings and is all about trying to portray a winning garden. The 4 Flower Gardener is so focused on pondering her own garden and feelings, that she forgets others also have emotional highs and lows.

At the end of the day, gardeners in this triad trust their actions and see their garden as a task to be done.

## THINKING (5-6-7s)

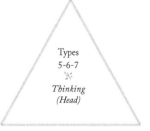

Also known as the *head* triad, individuals who reside in this group appear wise and knowledgeable, while often feeling dread inside.

The act of *thinking* for this gardener is taking the risk of acting on her thoughtfully designed garden plans. At some level, 5-6-7s are afraid that if they stop seeking information and perspective, they will never be prepared or find the answers they seek. Those in this triad are often described as *holding back* in that they display a need to step away from life and gain distance. As gardeners, 5-6-7s are all driven, at some level, by fear. Gaining perspective and planning is the name of the garden game! The 5 Flower Gardener externalizes her fear and relates to the garden through study and logic. The 6 Flower Gardener internalizes her fear and sees the garden through the lens of preparation and precaution. The 7 Flower Gardener forgets her fear and retreats into the realm of imagination and thoughts to plan a glorious garden.

At the end of the day, gardeners in this triad trust their thoughts and see their garden as a mystery to be understood.

### Instinct (8-9-1s)

Also known as the *gut* triad, individuals who reside in this group appear to be strong and invincible, while often holding a feeling of vulnerability inside. The concept of *instinctual energy* for these gardeners is to act on their gut feelings about their next garden quest. At some level, 8-9-1s are afraid that if they "let down their guard," they will lose control of themselves in one form or another. Those residing in this triad tend to have core issues around managing anger. In that sense, instinctual types are often described as *holding their ground*, in that they display a need to be firm and express their core, instinctual energy to hold on to their sense of self. As gardeners, 8-9-1s "self-forget" in some way or another: 8 Flower Gardeners overdo things until their body aches remind them that they forgot they are human! The 1 Flower Gardener forgets that all hoeing and weeding and no garden play makes for a very exhausting and un-fun garden existence. The 9 Flower Gardener forgets her own flower taste and garden views and merges with the garden ideas and plans of other gardeners.

At the end of the day, gardeners in this triad trust their judgments and see their garden as a battle to be won.

> *Come forth into the light of things,*
> *let nature be your teacher.*
> William Wordsworth

## ARROWS (PATHS) AND WINGS

When you look at the Enneagram diagram (page xvi), you will see that each number has a line that connects the type with four other numbers, one on each side, called *wings*, and the other two connected via *arrows*. The specific numbers that are connected to a particular type are associated with characteristics that provide opportunities for growth. While your core number will never change, these other four numbers provide the movement opportunity to flourish and become more resourceful.

## FOLLOW THE ARROWS (PATHS)

The arrows of the Enneagram are, in large part, what allow the Enneagram to guide us and make this particular typology so profound. While there are countless personality assessments that tell us who we *are*, the Enneagram arrows provide us with an awareness of how we can come to realize the qualities to which we might *aspire*—to be a resourceful, more resilient version of ourselves. Perhaps equally, if not more importantly, the Enneagram arrows also provide insight into when we may have lost our way, and guide us on the directions to regain a balance in our lives. In essence, the Enneagram typology is a *personality dance* that allows an individual to expand her repertoire of behavior in new and dynamic directions. In this book, in deference to the parlance of the garden, we will call the arrows, *paths*.

And, just when you thought—*I've got it! These arrows are cool!*—there's an even more insightful aspect to the arrows. In general, a particular type can follow the arrow/path to either connected type to draw from the energy and characteristics of that type. But there's a bit of a twist to this dance. When we are overly tired or on the edge, when the deer eat every last snowball hydrangea, we are in a less secure period in life. While in this stressful state, our personality tends to move in the direction of the arrow pointing *away* from our core number (see diagram, below). When we arrive, while we have an opportunity to incorporate the multitude of strengths and challenges of that particular type, we have an inclination to absorb and portray some of the *less beneficial* qualities of that connected type. However, the wisdom of the Enneagram guides us to stretch and draw from the more resourceful qualities of that type as well.

A garden example of this might be that, under stressful conditions, the 7 Flower Gardener moves in the direction of the arrow toward Type 1. When the Type 7 tumbles down the path to the flower garden of the

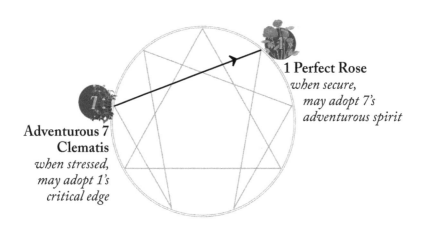

**1 Perfect Rose**
*when secure,*
*may adopt 7's*
*adventurous spirit*

**Adventurous 7**
**Clematis**
*when stressed,*
*may adopt 1's*
*critical edge*

Type 1, they are likely stressed out already and become even more so! In this 7/1 flower garden, the 7 Flower Gardener risks losing her imaginative, playful garden style, becoming instead critical—adopting a much less colorful and perhaps black-and-white garden palate. What a state she will find herself in, without any clues about how to regain her hues! However, if the 7 can stretch and shift perspective, she has the opportunity to absorb a more refined and vivid focus—the strengths of the Type 1 personality.

In contrast, when we are *on our game*, as in "our winter garden quince are all in full bloom," we tend to be in a less stressful, more secure period in life. In this space, our personality tends to move against the direction of the arrow pointing *toward* our core number. When we arrive, while we have an opportunity to incorporate the multitude of strengths and challenges of that particular type, we have a tendency to absorb and portray some of the *more beneficial*, resourceful aspects of that connected type.

A garden example of this might be that the 1 Flower Gardener walks swiftly down the path to the flower garden of the Type 7 when they are feeling garden bliss! In this 1/7 flower garden, the 1 Flower Gardener might let go of the perfect plot and sow wildflowers, just to play with the possibilities. The Type 1 Gardener at her best becomes mischievous—perhaps planting some rambling roses or climbing jasmine. Now, they won't go crazy—don't expect the Type 1 Gardener to plant *invasives* (oh my!), but perhaps a non-native, just for fun! Who knows, they might even consider letting "volunteer" wildflowers emerge in unexpected places!

In the end, in life and garden, what one experiences as stress or security will differ widely from one person to another. In the garden, stress may bring out the *best* in one and the *beast* in another. Similarly, a life season that is relaxed and secure may drive negative behaviors for some and desirable behaviors for others. I would suggest that the best way to think about the Enneagram stress/security arrows is to view them as pathways that provide insight into your core thoughts, feelings, and actions.

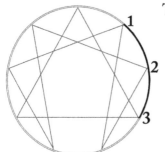

This diagram highlights the wings of the Type 2 Gardener. The numbers on either side of the core number—in this case, 1 and 3—are called the *wings* of the 2. Not unlike true wings, these numbers provide us an opportunity to soar! On the Enneagram, characteristics of either wing can influence our core personality type—and we can use these characteristics to "lean on" when our core personality needs some support. Similar to the arrows, the specific numbers that scaffold the core can provide opportunities to thrive or deteriorate.

In the garden, one can think of the Enneagram wings in terms of a direction to lean, much as a flower with a more delicate constitution leans on another for support. This analogy calls to mind my beautiful Roguchi clematis, with its deep-purple, bell-shaped flowers clinging and climbing upon my snowball viburnum in late spring. The usually low-growing clematis takes on new heights and the snowball flowers of the hydrangea appear to be capped with small purple hats. What a lovely leaning-clinging transformation. As an Enneagram Type 2, I envision myself as a Roguchi clematis leaning toward my ambitious Type 3 wing to put my own needs in the forefront and achieve new heights!

## CHANGING THE HUE OF YOU

One needs to wander no farther than the winter garden to witness the concept of changing hue. The hellebore (Lenten or winter rose) is and will always be a hellebore, of the family *Ranunculaceae*. A winter blooming, shade-loving, robust plant with muted shades of violet, green, or white cup-shaped flowers, the hellebore is widely grown and enjoyed. However, there are approximately twenty species, and while at core they share key characteristics, their hues, leaf patterns, and shapes may differ widely. Depending on climate, soil conditions, and other factors, every hellebore manifests different characteristics and hues that allow it to survive and thrive.

Like the hellebore, an individual type may need to, at times, enhance personality qualities to be a more hearty, robust, or vivid version of herself; or in contrast, to become more subdued. As in the garden, we may appear to be a different *species* or a hybrid version of ourselves for protection or resilience—but at core we are our own unique personality type.

Remarkably, if you place the hellebore flower with its muted shades of purple next to a scarlet-flamed dahlia or other vivid flower, the color of the hellebore will take on a slightly different appearance or shade. So, too, with the Enneagram—the wings on either side of the core number add a depth or dimensional characteristics that provide the opportunity to alter the core personality.

IN ESSENCE

*The flower offered of itself*
*And eloquently spoke*
*Of Gods*
*In languages of rainbows*
*Perfumes*
*And secret silence . . .*

Phillip Pulfrey

A well-recognized horticulturist, Gertrude S. Wister, wrote, "The flowers of late winter and early spring occupy places in our hearts well out of proportion to their size." Our flowers are our friends: we speak to them, nurture them, put them to bed in late October (okay, in August in upstate New York, but let's not quibble), and greet them in March with open (gloved) hands! But what some don't realize is that it isn't just their stunning show of colors that enriches our lives, but their intoxicating, bold, or ever-so-subtle scents—their very *essence*—that just might heal us.

Earlier in this chapter, you were introduced to the Enneagram typology concept of *divine essence* as the pure, core characteristics of our personality. However, over time, in order to cope, we develop compulsive personality patterns that cover up or deeply bury our divine essence. In the spirit of the garden, we look to Mother Nature to guide us to rediscover our divine essence; the motivation and energy of our core Enneagram type. We turn to garden flower essences as a unique way to literally awaken our senses to be the most healthy version of ourselves.

In brief, flower essences are made by infusing blossoms with a particular vibration into water and then stabilizing it. Sounds a little *out there*? Keep reading! There is wisdom that suggests that water has memory, and every flower has healing attributes that emit a vibrational frequency. The science behind all of this is *sympathetic resonance*. So, let's just act on the assumption that placing a unique-to-your Enneagram type, "helpful" blossom, into a pool (or bowl) of water will allow your mind and spirit to heal.

$$\frac{\text{Healing flower vibration + water memory}}{\text{Emotional imbalance vibrational frequency}} = \textbf{The Divine Essence of You!}$$

Well, just try one! The proof will be in your actions. I've read flower vibrations can be contagious, so go out and share some happiness, courage, and new-found confidence!

YOU DO NOT BECOME GOOD BY TRYING TO BE GOOD, BUT
BY FINDING THE GOODNESS THAT IS ALREADY WITHIN YOU,
AND ALLOWING THAT GOODNESS TO EMERGE.

ECKHART TOLLE

# 1. The Perfect Gardener
##  Rose

IN THE BEAUTIFUL line spoken by Juliet in Shakespeare's play *Romeo and Juliet*, "A rose by any other name would smell as sweet," Juliet argues that the names of things don't affect what they really are. Applying this to gardening, a Type 1—whether called a rose, iris, or phlox—will still maintain all of the cherished qualities of a rose, such as *perfection*. Likewise, the Type 1 Flower Gardener, no matter what title she carries in her life, will be the perfectionist, on a lifelong quest for rightness, her own and that of others. So, as you read about the attentive, conscientious, and proper Type 1 Flower Gardener, consider Romeo's response, "I take thee at thy word: call me but love, and I'll be new baptized; henceforth I never will be Romeo." You will come to know the elegant 1 Flower Gardener by following her graceful modeling of the "good and righteous" garden path.

# The Enneagram Type 1 Gardener Type Checklist

- I often think I could have done something better in my flower garden.
- I tend to focus on doing it "the right way," like purchasing native plants or using organic fertilizers.
- When I visit friends and their beautiful gardens, I reflect on what I could do better in my own garden.
- I think about becoming a master gardener or taking a class to improve my garden practices.
- I like an orderly garden.
- I take my garden seriously.
- I do *not* appreciate garden criticism. I try to garden correctly and am already hard enough on myself.
- In my garden, I often see the weeds rather than the flowers.
- Garden details are important to me and not to be overlooked.
- My running script is always how my garden could be improved.

If your response is *YES, YES, that's me*, you might identify as an Enneagram Type 1 Flower Gardener.

*Politeness is the flower of humanity.*
Joseph Joubert


## The Blossoms: The Strengths of the Type 1 Gardener

### Orderly and Organized Garden Bed

You'll know when you are in a healthy Type 1 flower garden. The flowers will literally be behaving! Type 1 Flower Gardeners have an outstanding eye for the errors other gardeners "pave over." Weeds? Never! Invasives? Not for long! Stones left *un*-turned? Are you kiddin'?! While most flower gardeners "get the job done," the 1 Flower Gardener doesn't leave a bed un-mulched. I'll bet my peonies on it! The attentive Type 1 will have a very organized, orderly flower bed:

- Mulch ordered
- Garden shed cleaned (oh yes, they not only have a shed, but they can *find* something *in* the shed!)
- Seeds ordered (on sale!)
- Plants arriving (in correct Zone)

Yes, the 1 Flower Gardener beds have sheets tucked and pillows plumped—ready for a very good night's sleep.

## THE PROPER PETAL

Ergonomic tools, check! Organic fertilizers, check! Gloves FIT (what, no holes?), check! Welcome to Type 1 flower gardening! Oh ye who have mud in your nails, trowels with lose grips, gloves with no tips: you are *not* Ones! Type 1s make wise, sensible choices in work and play, and those choices

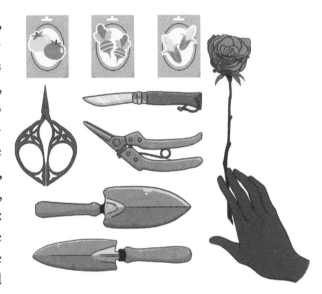

are reflected in their gardens. They will choose native and never invasive plants. You'll not only find compost, but most probably organic compost. Gardening is "serious business," and while they are loath to express a self-righteous attitude, let's face it: Gardening is a relationship with nature, to protect and improve the earth, and a 1 Gardener must be a good steward.

## The Diligent Digger

There is an old wives' tale of a
1 Flower Gardener who
was so focused on a
dragonfly perched
on a leaf that she
became covered in
English ivy and was
never seen again! Not
far from the truth, my
garden friends, because
Type 1s are focused! A 1
Flower Gardener, diligent
and focused, is rarely distracted

or off on a tangent, leaving a trowel here and a shovel there, while off watering dilapidated daisies! Nope. The 1 Gardener is *on it*, whatever *it* is, and will remain focused until the task is complete! Not unlike a novelist, the garden is the 1's great work, and they will edit, perfect, and re-work each row until their garden-novel is complete. The 1 flower garden would win the garden Pulitzer if there were such a prize. And when the Type 1 isn't working *in* the garden, she is thinking about what she might have missed, a plant placement here, or a shrub there—improvements, perfection, *everywhere*!

While the other Enneagram Flower Gardeners may (erroneously!) say—"My garden is perfect. Well done!"—the wise Type 1 observes and considers her garden a *work in progress*, and quietly reflects, "Next time, I already know the logical steps for enhancements!"

## The Conscientious Cultivator

Conscientious indeed! No easy way out for the 1 Flower Gardener. Their motto might be, "If you can't garden 'right' then get outta the garden!" Type 1s don't shirk responsibility in life, be it with family, friends, work, or hobbies. The 1 Flower Gardener gets excited when there isn't an aphid to be found in their rose bed. They are quite pleased with a challenge, be it weeding those pesky day lilies or dividing a root ball the size of Manhattan. And if/when they lose their cool with their garden helpers—I promise they'll accept their share of responsibility, apologize, and dig back in to get the job done. And with their extra time (by the light of the moon) you'll find the exhausted Type 1 making medicinal remedies with their echinacea, to share with their kid's third-grade class! Oh my.

## THE WEEDS: THE CHALLENGES FOR THE TYPE 1 GARDENER

In the 1 Flower Gardener's pursuit of being a conscientious, responsible gardener, she may find she has wandered a bit too far—and perhaps before realizing it, she has exaggerated her special garden talents. Having strayed into the weeds and brambles, the Type 1 finds herself being a garden-monitor or self-appointed garden critic.

Type 1s, perhaps more than their eight other petal'd friends, will get frustrated when their garden doesn't behave. You may not see their frustration, as Ones will keep their garden-grumbles below the surface. However, they may voice, "Despite my amended soil and organic fertilizer, my hydrangea is not producing the copious purple blossoms of yesteryear." You, the observer, are viewing *huge purple blossoms*! This is the unfortunate lens of a 1 Gardener entering into the weeds.

Let's explore a few of the Type 1 Flower Gardener's scratches and rashes, and then move forward to pathways out of the weeds!

### GUILTY AS GROWN

Oh dear. Talk about fertile ground for guilt. That's the lot (or is it plot?) of the 1 Flower Gardener: try as she might, she rarely lives up to her own expectations, nor does her garden. She might lament, "Why did I ever start this garden? I might as well let the bamboo take over the lawn and be done with it." The Type 1 will express that there is never, no, not *ever*, enough time, energy, or talent to grow the garden in her mind.

All the while, when you visit, you are thinking, "This flower garden looks like Monet's garden, but what do I know?" She may be resistant to your praise, but don't let that stop you from telling her so!

### THE HYPER-CRITICAL HORTICULTURIST

I know a 1 Flower Gardener who was corrected on her pronunciation of her delicate, threading clematis vine (the Type 1: CleMATis; the "former" friend: CLEMatis). She shared this with me as you would share that you murdered your neighbor's pet rabbit—red-faced and *sotto voce*. Her shame related to her mispronunciation, and she will never forget the humiliation (nor the pronunciation of clematis). The 1 Gardener may correct your garden choices or pronunciation and will assume others are checking on hers, also. However, I beg you not to correct a Type 1 in public—especially at the master gardeners' monthly luncheon roundtable.

The 1 Flower Gardener is her own task-master, and her garden path to recovery is to acknowledge and tolerate a *few* garden weeds. Who knows, one of those weeds might even be a perfect trillium in disguise!

### THE PEEVED PLANTER

Everyone has stopped by the 1 Flower Gardener's beautiful flower garden and openly acknowledged that she is a slam dunk for the garden of the year. But on the day of the announcement, she hears, "And the Garden of the Year goes to: the Mayor's garden." (*That* little, simple patch of common varietals?!)

While the "in-control" Type 1 will likely not *lose it*, she may readily admit feeling resentment for not being recognized. What could be a greater offense? Especially if the award committee awarded an inferior garden or (horror of horrors) a lazy, unconscientious gardener.

Type 1 Gardeners in life and the garden work so very hard, at basically every task they set about to accomplish. They will think nothing of burning the midnight citronella oil to prepare for the garden competition! To lose the award to a superior gardener—that she can handle, but if there's something amiss—watch out! A disgruntled 1 Gardener is not someone with whom I'd want to get into the garden brambles.

*There is simply the rose; it is perfect*
*in every moment of its existence.*
Ralph Waldo Emerson

## Knowing When the Type 1 Is in the Brambles (Turn Back!)

When the 1 Flower Gardener begins to lose control, and it seems that everything has "gone south"—that spells trouble. No matter how much she weeds, she can't seem to get ahead—it's hopeless! A voice in her head says, "What's the use? You'll never be a true flower gardener. You have a blue thumb."

Oh dear. You are overwhelmed with it all! Your flower garden now seems a *mess*. Perhaps if you just work harder! Up at dawn and still weed'n at dusk. Not enough!

At such times, the 1 Gardener might find herself careening down the path toward the arrow and the melancholy side of the Type 4 flower garden. Her anger turns on her, and she feels like a poor, pitiful petunia. This path is unfortunately full of brambles or (oh no!) dreaded English *and* poison ivy. If you are nearby, encourage the Type 1 to view the sunnier side of the 4 garden, which provides just the opportunity for the One to recognize that she can express her emotions and perhaps befriend her inner garden critic!

This may require a reframing of her garden image, realizing it doesn't have to be poison ivy *or* a prize rose. In the garden there is always fertile ground in-between. Courage, my Type 1! Continue to wind your way along the paths in the resourceful, beautiful, unique part of the Type 4 garden—there, the orchids will mesmerize and perhaps awaken that resourceful 1/4 combo of reality-based diligence, plus 4 Flower Gardener creativity. What a garden fusion that would be to behold!

> *But he that dares not grasp the thorn*
> *should never crave the rose.*
> Anne Brontë

## How to Find Your Path "Home"

Type 1 Flower Gardeners can not only thrive, they can flourish, and a fulfilling journey is to follow the path to the adventurous flower gardens of the 7 Flower Gardener. Notice I intentionally wrote gardens (plural), as a Type 7 will rarely stop at just one tantalizing garden bed (see Chapter 7 for more fun). The path from the 1 Flower Gardener to the 7 Flower Gardener isn't always easy, but you can do it, One!

When 1 Flower Gardeners journey to the 7 gardens, they can let their burdens of responsibility, critique, and intensity go—and find themselves in a garden of joy and playfulness. In the 7 garden, the Type 1 can allow their garden dreams to overflow into new spaces, without control or fear of a GARDEN-GONE-WILD! The 1 Flower Gardener can practice not being perfect! She can believe, "I'd rather be a very good gardener and have a blast!"

This resourceful 1/7 garden has no *shoulds*; rather, lots of garden *coulds*! Just imagine what the Type 1 might discover when she lets her garden- and life-critic rest awhile—perhaps a stunning 1/7 garden performance! It's a sunny day, so cheers to Type 1! Play, dear One, play!

## The Meaning of the Rose

The rose has many meanings, which vary depending on its color. Several resonate with the qualities of the Enneagram Type 1, including wisdom, devotion, and confidentiality. However, the rose was chosen as the flower for the Type 1 because of the beautiful perfection, albeit surrounded by thorns. There might be nothing more perfect than a single rose in a bud vase.

Nevertheless, if the rose flower is a bit too prickly for you, perhaps consider these other Type 1 Flower Gardener favorites (also see the Appendix).

**Coneflower**: Known for its native medicinal qualities and a seed provider for birds.

**Butterfly Weed**: Attracts hummingbirds and hordes of butterflies, bees, and other beneficial insects and serves as a food-source host plant for monarch butterflies to lay their eggs.

**Goldenrod**: Well, some people might not realize how special this plant is, until they know the health benefits.

**Sunflower**: Where soil pollution is high, sunflowers may be planted in order to help clean up the environment.

## In Essence: Crabapple

A little flower essence can help us soothe the pricks of thorns. For the 1 Flower Gardener, crabapple flower essence might do the trick! The Type 1 reading this might be thinking, "Oh, *right*, crabapple—thanks a lot!"

To that I respond, "Crabapple is *exactly* what you need!" Crabapple flower essence is known for its qualities to assist the Type 1 Flower Gardener to overcome perfectionism and encourage acceptance of herself and others.

With approximately fifty species of crabapple trees and bushes in the Northern Hemisphere, you're sure to find more than one *crabby apple* flower that will please you. It is said that if you add a little beech tree essence, you'll be even less tough on yourself. Who knew! Perhaps, you?

### DISTINCTIVE HUES OF THE ONE FLOWER GARDENER

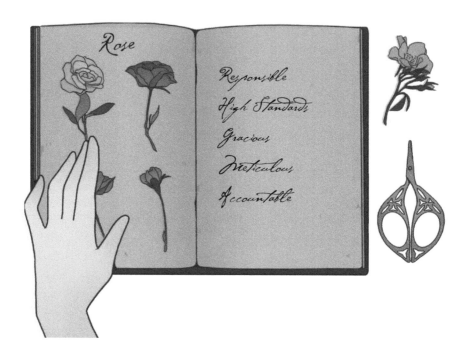

*I am only one, but I am one.*
*I cannot do everything, but I can do something.*
*And I will not let what I cannot do*
*interfere with what I can do.*
Edward Everett Hale

**Tips for the Type One Gardener**

- Take time to smell the June roses.
- *Perfect* is the enemy of the *so lovely*—your garden will never be perfect, so chill out.
- When your garden-critic whispers, take a trowel, dig a hole, and bury those words.
- Resist the urge to ask your garden helpers for "do-overs," if their work isn't up to your standards.
- The weeds will be there tomorrow, so lean on your 9 wing to relax, or take the path to 7 to play.
- Real gardeners make mistakes—and they forgive themselves.
- Try to accept garden criticism without defensiveness.
- Pick up a garden hobby in which you aren't perfect but that is fun.

My work is loving the world.
Here the sunflowers,
there the hummingbird—
equal seekers of sweetness.

Mary Oliver

## 2. The Helpful Gardener
### 🌿 Zinnia

WHILE THEIR WING, the 1 Flower Gardener, is all about perfection, the 2 Flower Gardener is quite proud of her ability to help the Type 1 achieve that perfection! Their song, to the tune of the woodchuck rhyme, goes:

*How much help would a Type 2 give*
*if a Type 2 could help you?*

Oodles! Regardless of her own needs, the Two is there for you. Known for their helpful and thoughtful nature, 2 Flower Gardeners just want to give of themselves and be appreciated in return.

As a Type 2 myself, I'll share one of my favorite poems, which also reflects a Two characteristic. It was written for me on my February birthday, coinciding by chance with the bloom of our first spring daffodil—which was in a bud vase next to the bed when I awoke that morning.

*Some men give diamonds, some give a ring.*
*But for you, my dear, Angela,*
*I give you spring!*

Just sayin'—it doesn't take jewels to make a 2 Flower Gardener's heart sing. Just a daffodil and a love note.

## The Enneagram Type 2 Gardener Type Checklist

- I often wish I had more time in my garden beds.
- I focus on what I can share from my garden to yours.
- When I visit friends and their beautiful gardens, I think about getting cuttings or divisions.
- I think about becoming a master gardener or taking a class to meet others and learn.
- I tend to overdo and perhaps help others even when my help was not requested.
- I like others to visit and appreciate my flower garden.
- I am disappointed when visitors don't enjoy and say nice things about my garden.
- There is always a new project to do in my garden.
- I'm exhausted. I can't keep up with all of the "to-do's" in life and my garden.
- I enjoy advising on plants for friends' gardens.

If your response is *YES, YES, that's me*, you might identify as a Type 2 Gardener.

*Flowers always make people better, happier, and more helpful;*
*they are sunshine, food, and medicine for the soul.*
Luther Burbank

## THE BLOSSOMS: THE STRENGTHS OF THE TYPE 2 GARDENER

### THE SUPPORTIVE SPROUT

You'll know when you are in a healthy Type 2 flower garden. The flowers are literally supporting each other as if to say, "Lean on me, when your bloom is too heavy." Type 2 Flower Gardeners are not only busy in their own garden, they will stop in their garden tracks to help you with *your* garden, and *her* garden, and the *community* garden!

The true 2 Flower Gardener is knowledgeable and will provide transplants for the novice gardener and will probably dig, transplant, and re-plant seedlings in your garden while you sip on your mint julep.

Too much? Perhaps, but if you need someone to assist you, look over your fence and find yourself a Type 2 Gardener.

### THE COMFORTABLE GARDEN BED

Type 2s are all about appearance and showing you just how nice it is to visit in their garden. Yes, the 2 Flower Gardener strives to make the garden experience "just right"! Is a bed too cold? Have an extra blanket of mulch! Too firm? How about a soft-bed of amended soil! Now your garden is ready for a very good winter sleep.

A 2 Flower Gardener just gets everyone's needs, and then they will show you how much they care! The Type 2 garden might not be a secret garden, but it will be a haven to "sit a spell" and talk. If there is space, there is likely a nook *and* a cranny, with comfortable lawn chairs—and the 2 Flower Gardener will give you the better lawn chair! Not enough?

How about a cool beverage? Soft music? Just make sure you say, "Ahhh, this is so lovely!" Because for all of her do-ing, the Type 2 wants and longs for love and appreciation. And I can almost promise that, for your appreciation, you'll be rewarded with a bouquet, seedlings, and promise of the next garden sleepover.

## THE GENEROUS GARDENER

Twos are all about going the extra mile, especially for those with whom they have a relationship. That could mean thousands of folks, given that 2s have a way of making and keeping friends. If flowers are the language of love, 2 Flower Gardeners have a field of blooming hearts. They will create a lovely atmosphere for helpers and garden friends—whether in their own little plot of dirt or a community garden. A 2 Flower Gardener will have your back, and if you hoe their row, they'll weed yours. Twos will replace your picket fence and consult with you on what might be ailing your wilting daisies, all while making a light lunch. No matter what the chore, you can be sure a 2 will sweat right alongside you.

## THE CREATIVE CULTIVATOR

Twos are all about looking attractive, and that also applies to their garden beds, buds, and blossoms. In general, Type 2s want to surround themselves with a garden that they enjoy and others will like—with nice touches such as bird feeders, a little bubbling fountain, stone walls, a violinist playing Vivaldi (well, okay, they *would* if they *could*). Oh yes, and lighting—solar, of course! The 2 Flower Gardener is generous as well as nurturing and wants nothing more than to cultivate a space that speaks to and highlights her best qualities.

> *Gardeners are good at nurturing,*
> *and they have a great quality of patience.*
> *They're tender. They have to be persistent.*
> Ralph Fiennes

## The Weeds: The Challenges for the Type 2 Gardener

In the 2 Flower Gardener's pursuit of being a helpful, problem-solving gardener, she may find she has helped herself to the wrong gardens. Perhaps before realizing it, she has exaggerated her special garden talents. Having strayed into the weeds and brambles, the Type 2 finds she has helped herself to, let's just say, spaces UN-invited. Let's explore a few of the Two's wrong turns and then move forward to pathways out!

### Exhausted Ephemeral

Oh, for the love of Peat—why can't some gardeners ask for help? Very difficult to understand for the busy, over-committed, "never met a friend or flower I didn't love" 2 Flower Gardener. If the 2 Gardener stops to actually smell the roses, or God forbid, take a nap in her hammock (*what?!*), she might actually get in touch with her own needs and feelings. So instead, she just keeps on moving rocks, building arches, and weeding. And when she tires of working in her own garden, the Type 2 will move right into yours. If the Two takes a moment of rest after all of the aforementioned chores, she may let her nearest and dearest friends hear about how the day's tasks were grueling. And in a moment of utter and complete exhaustion, she may even accept help from your garden-gloved hand! But don't hold your breath waiting for the Type 2 Flower Gardener to tell you what she needs—you'll likely end up violet-blue before she talks!

## UNAPPRECIATED IVY

Twos love nothing more than visitors stopping by their garden. However, when you don't appreciate their garden, it can get ugly. While the 2 Flower Gardener may not say it to your face, they'll say it to their housemate, or the cat or the dog: "Wow! _____ (insert name of ungrateful former friend) didn't even notice the lilies or the little path with the wild roses or how everything is in full bloom." Not hearing a compliment is such a bummer for the 2 Flower Gardener. She can then move quickly from feeling unappreciated to being a garden martyr. "Geez, all the plants I've shared and ogled in _____'s (insert name of same ungrateful friend) garden, and frankly, it is sooo overgrown." You get the picture. Resourceful 2s can hopefully dig out of this over-trodden path and garden for the love of their own little piece of earth. But just in case, the next time you visit a bloomin' 2 garden, you will be asked to choose any of the following responses to her very simple, multiple-choice questionnaire:

**Possible Responses to a Type 2's
"Do-You-Like-My-Garden" Rating Scale:**

    a.  I love your garden SO much
    b.  I SO love your garden
    c.  All of the above

## OVER THE TOP OF THE TRELLIS

I know a Type 2 Gardener who suggested to her husband that she place a sign out in front of her cutting garden all summer that read, "Flowers! Cut a Bouquet and Pay!" This creative Two thought she would have scissors (with a bow, of course) and little ties for the flower bundles and a decorative "pay bucket." It wasn't until her husband reminded her that, after the first five cars stopped in May, there would likely be no more flowers to pick. Let alone for her to enjoy in vases in her own house all summer! Ah, the 2 Gardener trap! She is so busy *giving* that the Two ends up with a dandelion/wild onion bouquet for herself. Perhaps better to nibble a wild green salad?

The Type 2 in life and garden tends to be overly helpful—to the point of literally giving away the farm! The Two can also be prone to providing unsolicited garden advice. A note to Type 2: tend to your own garden plot; others can turn over their soil just fine without you. And we love you no matter what you do—most importantly, be true to your authentic Two.

## Knowing When the Type 2 Is in the Brambles (Turn Back!)

When the 2 Flower Gardener hits the proverbial garden rock wall, there may be tears (well, walls *do* hurt) and bruised feelings. After immersion in all of the *doing* and *giving*, the Type 2 will be exhausted and not in touch with what she needs to nurture herself. At these times, she might find herself hurtling down the path toward the intolerant side of the 8 flower garden. She might cease to be a garden helper, and if she is really in the mud, she might even sling a little toward those who snub all of her efforts. This is the Type 2, where the *just-don't-appreciate* bloom is definitely off of the rose, and if offenders get too close they will feel the sting of sharp thorns (hopefully, before it gets too bloody).

Yet, in this same 8 garden, 2 Gardeners can get in touch with their need for a nice picket fence and stand in their own two garden clogs! In those sturdy shoes, the 2 Gardener can come to incorporate the hardy side of the 8 flower garden! In this vibrant 2/8 garden, the Type 2 can rely on herself, taking into account her own gut instincts and needs. In this flower garden, the Type 2 moves out of her garden comfort zone and connects to her personal flower-power, expressing anger and emotion with less regard about how others react. In this space she might just cut a big bouquet of sunflowers for her *own* vases—and let the sun shine down on one and only beautiful, talented, Two!

> *We need to do a better job of putting ourselves*
> *higher on our own "to do" list.*
> Michelle Obama

## How to Find Your Path "Home"

The Two Flower Gardener can GROW—and the most fulfilling path is to follow the garden path to the unique and creative Type 4 garden. The path will require her to walk by herself, feeling oh-so-special, and she can do it! When 2 Gardeners journey to the 4 flower garden, they stop inviting others over the fence and get in touch with their own creativity and inner garden uniqueness. When the 2 Flower Gardener skips against the arrow on the path to the Type 4 garden, it is a wonder to behold—perhaps expressed in garden art or rare plants—with many sweet surprises.

There are no demands or expectations for appreciation in this 2/4 dynamic. When the 2 Flower Gardener finds herself in this space, she will feel the depths and ecstasy of what a true garden has to offer. Be still, Two, and enjoy the magic!

## The Meaning of the Zinnia Flower

The zinnia flower has several meanings, including thoughts of friends, endurance, daily remembrance, goodness, and lasting affection. The zinnia reminds us of matters of the heart. Pick a bouquet for a vase of happiness.

If the zinnia flower is a bit too perky for you, perhaps consider these other 2 Flower Gardener favorites (also see the Appendix):

**Geranium**: Symbolizes true friendship and is super comforting.

**Tickseed**: Just as cheerful as can be.

**Butterfly Bush**: A butterfly magnet!

**Forget-Me-Not**: Every Type 2's request.

## In Essence: Chicory

The aroma of flowers can be intoxicating! So why not try a little essence to help us out? For the Type 2 Flower Gardener, chicory might just do the trick. The 2 Flower Gardener reading this is thinking to herself, "I eat chicory, and I stop being exhausted. Bring it ON!"

To that I say, "Yes!" Chicory essence is known for its qualities to assist those who feel like what they do for people goes unappreciated. This little boost will also help you feel fulfilled in your acts of service by not expecting anything in return.

So, if you are feeling like a bummed-out 2 Flower Gardener, sip some chicory. Then forgive and (plant some) forget-me-nots!

*Each flower is a soul*
*blossoming out to nature.*
Gérard de Nerval

## DISTINCTIVE HUES OF THE TWO FLOWER GARDENER

Zinnia

Responsive

Helpful

Generous

Perceptive

Problem-solver

**Tips for the Type Two Gardener**

- Take time in your own garden.
- Find a time and place to explore creativity in your garden and life.

- When you feel the urge to help or rescue, reflect on whether it is your interest alone.
- Practice random acts of anonymous giving and service.
- Trim back—on *everything*!
- Practice self-care; it's not selfish, it's essential.
- Question yourself when you are trying too hard to win the approval of another.
- Don't just say "Yes"; try, "I'll think about it and get back to you." "No" is also recommended.

THE GLORY OF GARDENING: HANDS IN THE DIRT,
HEAD IN THE SUN, HEART WITH NATURE.
TO NURTURE A GARDEN IS TO FEED
NOT JUST THE BODY, BUT THE SOUL.

ALFRED AUSTIN

## 3. The Efficient Gardener
### ❧ Hollyhock

THERE'S SLEEPY AND Dopey, Doc and Sneezy, Grumpy and Happy, Bashful and Busy! Wait a minute? Eight dwarfs? Yes, Snow White and Disney literally forgot to mention the eighth dwarf: Busy, the 3 Flower Gardener! The easily hummed tune of the well-known Disney song is literally the theme song for the Type 3 Gardener! Hum along:

> *Hi Ho, Hi Ho, it's off to work we go!*
> *We dig dig dig with a shovel or a stick*
> *We dig dig dig up everything in sight,*
> *We take our time then find some more!*
> *There's thousands to be some time born.*
> *And we don't know what we dig them for!*
>
> *We dig dig dig-a-dig dig!*
> Snow White and the Eight Dwarfs

Type 3 Flower Gardeners are just busy people, humming along, getting all kinds of garden and *life* things accomplished while the rest of us sloths are drinking our first cuppa joe and considering what we might tackle with a shovel or a hoe. To the Three, it is a *full-on, twenty-four-hour work day*! Rest? Pshaw—only after those pesky weeds are eradicated and the flower bed is tilled. As the sun sets and the Type 3 has made a pot of fresh verbena tea, she finally calls it a day. Sleep well, Three, your work is done. At least for the night.

## The Enneagram Type 3 Gardener Type Checklist

- I love double-duty flowers that are beautiful and useful.
- I like colorful blooms, with a lot of bang for the buck.
- When I visit other gardens, I look for horticulture tips and flowers to use in my own garden.
- I take courses so I can immediately use the information to enhance my garden.
- Less work and more flowers is my motto. I have lots of stuff going on.
- I am an efficient gardener, if nothing else.
- My garden might not *be* perfect, but it *looks* perfect.
- I tend to compete with other gardeners.
- I don't spend a lot of time relaxing in my garden.
- My running script is, "What is my next garden project?"

If your response is *YES, YES, that's me,* you might identify as a Type 3 Flower Gardener.

*A garden requires patient labor and attention. Plants do not grow merely to satisfy ambitions or to fulfill good intentions. They thrive because someone expended effort on them.*
Liberty Hyde Bailey

## The Blossoms: The Strengths of the Type 3 Gardener

### "And the Winner Is . . ."

"Who, *me?!*" Says the humble Three! Welcome to the personality of a Type 3 Gardener. Her garden is a winner, and her flowers will beam and take a bow, with praise well deserved! Three Flower Gardeners will till, hoe, and weed their way to achieve the Garden Gold Ribbon prize. Call the Three competitive? You can bet on it! However, no lazy-daisy, the 3 Gardener will work by sun and moon to succeed. Image is everything! When most flower gardeners are sleeping, Type 3 is up with the rooster, and they should be allowed to crow about it! They have a way with words and images that will impress even the most harsh of garden judges.

Are you a Type 3 Flower Gardener? Well, answer these two questions: (1) Do you consider yourself an ambitious gardener? (2) Have you ever placed an entry in "Garden Winners" magazine? If your answer is no, the verdict is clear: you are not a Three!

## The Efficient Garden Bed

Okay, let's just face it: if you think you are a 3 Flower Gardener while *reading* this, you may not truly be a Type 3. Why? Any self-respecting 3 Gardener has already downloaded this book as an audiobook to listen to while she is weeding! And when she isn't in the garden, the Three is reading up on "How to Grow Beauties in Record Time!" or "How to Plan a High-Yield Flower Bed." The Type 3 doesn't shy away from digging, mulching, or weeding—in fact, she might over-do. But don't be fooled, with all of the demands on their time and energy, the 3 Gardener will be the first to pay the neighbor's twelve-year-old to weed for summer spending money! Yes, the Three's flower bed will likely double as a sofa or potting shelf, with multi-purpose sheets and a plump pillow of weed-discouraging mulch—at the ready for a quick catnap before getting back to work (in the garden, of course)!

## The Dynamic Digger

The sign at the gate of a Type 3 garden reads, "*Gardening for the Ambitious. Amateurs Need Not Apply!*" The 3 Gardener is a little like poison ivy (nooo, not itchy!)—she is contagious, with an energetic personality that can motivate a garden-team in no time flat. The Type 3 will leave no stone unturned (literally) and, despite yourself, she will have you rock-turning right alongside her! The dynamo Three will post the garden list on the fence, and while the rest of us laggards make a list and *lose* it, Type 3s make a list and *use* it! If you say, "cannot," the 3 Flower Gardener will respond with "why not?" So if there is a Three in the garden, get outta' her way—or pick up your trowel, if you're going to stay!

## The Productive Pollinator

Just a garden? *Au contraire!* The Three's flower garden is a *jardin extraordinaire!* The industrious 3 Flower Gardener can market, manage, and publicize a garden to a stump—and the stump will listen up! You say "*patch* of flowers," the 3 Flower Gardener says "*quilt* of blossoms"; you say "*garden bed*," the 3 Flower Gardener says "*canopy of blooms*." The concept of garden productivity takes on a whole new meaning to the Type 3. Doing one task at a time is for wimps—and the Three will show you how multitasking is done. If you want to achieve your wildest garden dreams, find yourself a 3 Gardener!

> *We are so accustomed to wearing a disguise*
> *before others that eventually we are*
> *unable to recognize ourselves.*
> Francois de La Rochefouchauld

## The Weeds: The Challenges for the Type 3 Gardener

In the 3 Flower Gardener's pursuit of being an efficient, industrious flower gardener, she may find she has helped herself to being the chair of the garden committee. Perhaps, *every* committee! Having strayed into the weeds and brambles, the Three finds she has wheedled her way into too much territory and doesn't know how to find her way home. Let's explore a few of the wrong turns the Type 3 makes, and then move forward to pathways out of the weeds.

### The Unmindful Meadow

The Type 3 meadow will be thick with flowers and yield abundant bouquets—a result of the Three's hard work. Yet, ask a 3 Flower Gardener *who they are* as a gardener, and you might find yourself with a single blossom—or abandoned in the weeds. The 3 Gardener will be at the ready to share their goals, accomplishments, and practical tips. But Type 3s struggle with being *still* in most aspects of their lives—including in a lush meadow or cottage garden. In order to find herself in the garden and life, the Type 3 must stop doing and start being. That requires her to slow down to smell the flowers and dig deep, inside herself.

### The Boastful Blossom

Three Flower Gardeners have *a lot* to boast about, but humility isn't their strong suit. How will you know the achievements of a 3 Flower Gardener? Uh, duh: just listen! Type 3s will share their achievements like dropping a trail of breadcrumbs on the path—ever so subtly, but clearly in view. And don't you dare step on them! If you've never seen a garden acronym, try looking at the 3 Flower Gardener's signature line. It will read, GOT-YA (Gardener of the Year, Always!), with an MBA (Most

Blossoms Award). Unfortunately, Three Gardeners can be their worst garden enemy when they don't recognize that nobody likes a garden-boaster. When a Three sings their own praises too loudly, the very people the 3 Gardener wants to impress put plugs of mint in their ears. Note to the Type 3: perhaps plant some Humil-It Tea.

## THE PICTURE-PERFECT PATCH

Image is everything! Just ask a 3 Flower Gardener. Threes know that a picture paints a thousand words, and if you don't believe me, just take a look on their social media site—you'll see. And to learn about how to present your garden's best beds or the perfect time of day to have that garden-committee walkabout, just turn to a happy-to-advise Type 3 (most likely a small business owner of Show Your Best Garden, Inc.). A bit of a show-off, perhaps, or a smart gardener who knows how to highlight the blossoms and stash weeds under a bushel basket. Just don't peek in the garden shed with its lovely brass padlock. The wise Three knows where to hide the rusty garden hoe and un-presentable pots. Do not trespass!

*Software is like gardening—one day I'll go behind the shed
and clean up. But if nobody ever goes there,
does it matter a lot?*
Mike Krieger

## Knowing When the Type 3 Is in the Brambles (Turn Back!)

Oh dear. Your clematis isn't climbing and the deer nibbled your last hydrangea! "Who cares?" thinks the weary-worn 3 Flower Gardener. "I might as well fill the whole bed with pebbles and go watch *Forrest Gump*." When a stressed 3 Flower Gardener is done, *done*, **done**, that's what it sounds like. Instead of trusting her natural 3 Flower Gardener competence and innate garden-gumption, she throws in the trowel.

When the Three is dealt a bad plant or a scourge of aphids—she starts to secretly hope for a very early frost (so what if it's June?). Rather than deal with the problem, she may find herself running in the direction of the arrow down the path to the un-resourceful side of the 9 Flower Gardener. In this 3/9 garden space, she will distract or procrastinate herself right out of the whole, darn garden business. Instead of reaching inside herself to tap the wisdom of her inner-garden guru, she will doubt herself and seek external solutions.

There is hope, though, if the Type 3 can slow down enough to let the gentian, true-blue return! Gimme a "High-Nine"! This is the side of the 9 garden to which she needs to wander! When Threes find themselves in a hole, they must meander in this direction to find stillness and consider regaining some balance in life and garden activities. In this contemplative 3/9 garden, she can plant a peace lily and embrace all of the feelings that might sprout—and allow herself the time and space to let those feelings grow and bloom!

The 3 Flower Gardener can thrive, and the most fulfilling path is to walk against the direction of the arrow on the path to the prepared and loyal 6 Flower Gardener. The sign on the Type 6's gate reads, *Dear Three, Pass through and to Thine Own Self Be True!*

When the 3 Flower Gardener opens up to the energy of the Type 6 Flower Gardener, she is loyal to herself and others, rather than to her products and achievements. Maybe her Three flower garden isn't the award-winner or she doesn't become Gardener of the Month, but she learns to find contentment, hanging out with her own "buds"! In the 6 garden, she will learn to slow down and ponder some choices before digging. In the loyal garden of the Type 6, the 3 Flower Gardener dares to experience her feelings and doubts—and be settled in the uncertainty.

So, dear Three, lay your well-worn garden gloves down, and hand the hoe over to a friend—this is a 3/6 team effort.

## The Meaning of the Hollyhock Flower

Do not let its muted colors and delicate flowers fool you! This flower means ambition. Perhaps we should rename it the "Just Do It" flower! Hollyhock is tied to ambition because of the overall strength of the plant to grow in an array of conditions and its powerful presence in landscaping scenery.

If the hollyhock flower is a bit too elaborate for your taste, perhaps consider these other 3 Flower Gardener favorites (also see the Appendix):

**Bear's Breeches**: Represents artifice.

**Daphne Odora**: Ah! Fame and glory to the Daphne!

**Hydrangea**: You're so vain! You probably think this flower's about you!

**Phlox**: A workhorse in the garden, phlox will bloom all summer long, for quite the show.

> *The woods are lovely, dark and deep,*
> *but I have promises to keep,*
> *and miles to go before I sleep,*
> *and miles to go before I sleep.*

Robert Frost

## IN ESSENCE: DANDELION

The essence of flowers can be extremely useful. So why not try a little essence to help you get your mojo back? For the Three, dandelion flower essence might do the trick! The 3 Flower Gardener reading this is thinking, "I am not going to stop what I'm doing to sip on a *weed*!"

To that I respond, "Bow gently to this very useful blossom!" When the 3 Flower Gardener is on her game, she has enough energy to solo-staff a botanical garden! Forces of nature, Type 3s have dynamic physical energy and are a life force unto their own! But even the dynamic 3 Flower Gardener gets overwhelmed, and when she finds herself on her last garden ladder rung (over-striving/over-driving), it is time to stop and find her inner essence. Dandelion essence helps to release tension from the mental body and calm the senses, connecting one more fully with the present moment. How about a little dandelion tea?

*Learn to be quiet enough to hear the genuine in yourself,*
*so that you can hear it in others.*
Marian Wright Edelman

## DISTINCTIVE HUES OF THE
## THREE FLOWER GARDENER

### Tips for the Type Three Gardener

- Stop Doing. Start *Being* in your garden.
- Find hammock. Put down garden tools. Close eyes. Don't plan.
- Find a friend to walk your authentic garden path with you.

- Reflect on what gets sacrificed when you work in your garden too much.
- Your flowers and garden critters love you no matter what you do.
- Admit your garden disasters to at least one person.
- Practice some form of meditation in your garden daily.
- Notice and appreciate the birds and the bees in your garden.

AND FORGET NOT THAT THE EARTH DELIGHTS
TO FEEL YOUR BARE FEET AND
THE WINDS LONG TO PLAY WITH YOUR HAIR.

Khalil Gibran

## 4. The Aesthetic Gardener
### ❀ Orchid

VICTOR HUGO WROTE, "Melancholy is the happiness of being sad." Perhaps our friend Victor is a Type 4? I ask you, who titles a novel, *Les Miserables*, if not a Four?! The 4 Flower Gardener *does not garden like you and me*. Please commit that sentence to memory, because it is a very important distinction as it relates to the personality of the Type 4.

Fours are *special* Flower Gardeners, and they will let you know it one way or another. They *feel* their gardens and experience the ecstasy of every dew drop and intricate spider web on an early spring morning. I took a wild-flower identification class with a 4 Flower Gardener, and she said "thank you" to every tiny blossom she plucked for educational purposes. Unfortunately, I had inadvertently murdered a few on the trail before *I got with the program*. I apologized, I promise. But the message here is that 4 Flower Gardeners are very much in touch with both the agony and the ecstasy of life in the garden. And they also experience the garden (well, everything!) with a range of emotions. Read on—and enjoy the whirling, swirling dance of the 4 Flower Gardener.

# THE ENNEAGRAM TYPE 4
## GARDENER TYPE CHECKLIST

- My garden is anything but ordinary.
- I have a sense of the dramatic, whether in life or in my garden.
- I enjoy buying unique garden art and special, creative garden items.
- When I look over the *metaphorical garden fence* I'm often envious.
- When I visit friends and their beautiful gardens, I feel my garden isn't as nice.
- Deep down I don't think I'll ever be a *real* gardener.
- I am my moods, and experience ecstasy and defeat in my garden.
- I've been told I have a great eye for beauty, and that shows in my garden.
- When I feel good about myself, I feel good about my garden.
- I can spend hours on a garden bench listening to a friend who is hurting.

If your response is *YES, YES, that's me*, you might identify as a Four Flower Gardener.

> *Look, hasn't my body already*
> *felt like the body of a flower?*
> Mary Oliver

## THE BLOSSOMS: THE STRENGTHS
## OF THE TYPE 4 GARDENER

### ROMANCING THE GARDEN

*The scent is intoxicating, the colors mesmerizing! Whispers of poetry linger in the air: Rilke, Oliver, Wordsworth. Just beyond the rise, a gentle spray of water touches your face as if a garden fairy kissed you ever so gently.* Are you queasy reading these descriptions? Are you rolling your eyes? If so, you are *not* a 4 Flower Gardener! Type 4s are romantics, through and through, and they will express their thoughts and feelings. Don't be surprised if a 4 Flower Gardener begins to cry when she witnesses the way the sunlight illuminates a bumble bee moving gracefully on the blossoms of purple salvia. Emotion is a friend to the Four, and she may be deeply moved by what some gardeners barely give a glance. Type 4s are perhaps the most deeply creative gardeners of the nine of us. Sculptures and natural garden creations will be artistically presented in Type 4 garden spaces. Cross your fingers that the 4 Flower Gardener will invite you to join her in her garden, and swing open the gate into a space full of magical moments and deep emotions you never thought possible.

The Compassionate Garden Bed

You woke up this morning to a find your six-year-old daphne odora withering before your eyes! There is only one thing to do: call a 4 Flower Gardener—she will let you spill your tears while she gently massages your aching back. Fours just have a way of being *with* others in their times of sadness; they might even take your dead daphne and *sadness* home with them! In fact, while Type 4s deeply feel the elation of beauty, they aren't at all afraid to experience the depths of their own or others' despair. They want to be with the real you—and feel great empathy for others experiencing authentic emotion—in whatever form the emotion is presented. So, find a 4 Flower Gardener to whom you can rant, rave, and cry-a-river—she will come prepared with a box of tissues and a rowboat to ride out your sorrow.

INTUITIVE IRRIGATOR

It's as though the 4 Flower
Gardener has antennae that
are finely tuned to shifts in feelings
and the collective mood, not unlike how
a barometer senses a change in air pressure.
Now, I'm not saying you should call a Type
4 to decide if you need to cover your tender
perennials or inquire about an impending
drought! I did write, *antennae*, not a crystal ball. However, if any gardener is going
to be aware of shifting winds and moods—
it'll be a Four. They are very sensitive to
something being off—as they, themselves, always feel a
little off the beaten
path, acknowledging
that they are seeking something that
they lost and can't quite find. It's as
if Frances Hodgson Burnett knew a
4 Flower Gardener when she wrote,
"She had begun to wonder why she
had never seemed to belong to anyone."
In the end, the 4 Flower Gardener, while
incredibly intuitive, is desperately trying to
find herself.

## The Classy Cultivator

A tacky Type 4 garden? Not on my watch! Four Flower Gardeners are basically a "class-act." Unfortunately, they want you to notice their classiness—but I'll not go there in this section (see "The Weeds," below).

The 4 Flower Gardener can literally take what is ordinary and make it special—like the metamorphosis of the caterpillar into a butterfly. The Type 4 is the magician, and her garden is where the magic happens. When in the original garden of the 4 Flower Gardener, you will find the Midas touch everywhere you look—and they value and embrace the smallest snowdrop blossom in winter to the phoenix moth on the unfurling datura blossoms on a hot July night. If a flower garden is a natural museum, the garden of the Four is the Louvre. And the 4 Flower Gardener will welcome you with a seductive Mona Lisa smile.

*Embrace what makes you unique, even if it makes others uncomfortable. I didn't have to become perfect, because I've learned throughout my journey that perfection is the enemy of greatness.*
Janelle Monae

## The Weeds: The Challenges for the Type 4 Gardener

### Desiring the Unattainable

Perhaps you have read John Milton's epic poem, *Paradise Lost*—where Adam and Eve lost *eternal spring with the changing seasons and ended up with storms, winds, hail, ice, floods, and earthquakes.* Not good, folks. In brief, they lost bliss and ended up spending their life trying to regain paradise. Not to be melodramatic—even though our 4 Flower Gardeners

don't particularly mind melodrama—
but Type 4s feel much like these two:
something special was taken from
them, and they are not only bummed,
but they are in perpetual pursuit of finding
paradise once again. I do wonder if
Milton was a Type 4.

What the Four wouldn't give
for "that" garden or "those flowers"—the paradise *just over there.*
Perhaps you might perceive by now
that 4 Flower Gardeners struggle with
desiring the unavailable. The flower garden that the
Type 4 *has* is suddenly not what she *wants*, and the
garden she *wants* is likely in a universe far, far away.
The Four truly believes that there is a Shangri-La, and she
is on a perpetual quest to find it: through a partner, a place,
a journey, or perhaps, a flower garden. If only 4 Flower
Gardeners could come to realize that the most beautiful
blooms are inside them. Paradise, *found.*

## A Shovel-full of Drama

"This is my LIFE in a *nutshell,*" says the melodramatic 4 Flower Gardener,
after witnessing every last tulip bulb dug up by an industrious squirrel.
This is said as if the Four Gardener has been personally targeted by the
dastardly squirrel and his cronies. I once read the phrase that Type 4s don't
*have* feelings, they *are* their feelings! The 4 Flower Gardener has a bit of a
flair for the melodramatic, and they aren't shy about expressing it.

True confession: I told a fib the other day when facilitating an Enneagram workshop. A participant asked if there was a particular Enneagram

Type that is more self-deprecatory, and I said, "Absolutely not!" I suggested that the Enneagram is EOE (Equal Opportunity Enneagram), and all types can portray various emotional states, all the while knowing that, for this particular question, my response was, perhaps, untrue. KA-BOOM! Tossed out of the Garden of Eden!

Truth be told, I believe the Type 4 is a bit more prone to self-disparagement, because she struggles with her self-worth. A 4 Flower Gardener will be devastated when her calla lilies don't re-bloom after a harsh winter, or (God forbid) her prize edgeworthia up and dies. In true dramatic form over these losses, the Four will announce on social media that she is doomed to a brown-thumb or, worse, proclaim herself a plant murderer—and embark on a journey of self-reflection to heal her wounds. The next posted photos will be of the 4 Flower Gardener on an ashram, in a wild orchid garden, reading or re-creating her own version of Elizabeth Gilbert's book and movie, *Eat Pray Love.* Julia Roberts, step aside, because you don't hold a candle to a Type 4 taking the lead in her own dramatic role.

## Extra-special Floret

No offense or anything, but if you are characteristically chipper or eternally optimistic, I wouldn't count on being BFF with a 4 Flower Gardener. While a Four might *tolerate* you for a short while—they are looking for folks who understand the trials and tribulations of life, as well as the ecstasies, in and out of the garden. To a 4 Flower Gardener, a perpetually happy, cheery gardener is akin to a garden that is made up of only nandina. Horror of horrors. You see, Type 4s are in search of deep, authentic emotions, whether they be in a friend, life partner, or type of flower. They will very likely search far and wide to find the perfect sculptor or blacksmith to create their garden gate. They'll track down the boutique garden center that they found by sleuthing on the internet.

Fours are just attracted to the unique, rare, and extraordinary. They care deeply about meaningful subjects—so please, no trivial garden chitchat if you befriend a 4 Flower Gardener—be prepared to dig deep, or get outta their garden.

> *If you like a flower you pick it. If you love a flower*
> *you water it. Appreciation over possession.*
>
> Osho

## Knowing When the Type 4 Is in the Brambles (Turn Back!)

When the 4 Flower Gardener finds herself buying a pot of petunias at the local garden center, there is trouble ahead. To put it bluntly, petunias are ordinary, everybody has petunias—and the Type 4 wants to be exciting, and that goes for her garden, too. And when the Four feels that her garden and life are coming up petunias, she will either drum up some garden drama or introject her grief and tote her sadness around like a pail full of potting soil. Melancholy is a familiar friend to the 4 Flower Gardener, and if her garden isn't extraordinary, then she will spend her time yearning for that "yonder garden"—just over the hill.

At these times, the Type 4 might say, "What's the use? My garden skills are beyond redemption," and throw herself into the community garden. This can become a downhill path for the 4 Flower Gardener embracing the less-becoming aspects of the Type 2 flower garden. On this side of the 4/2 garden, there are mole holes full of martyrdom and repressed feelings. If possible, my dear Four, say sorry to the moles, put one foot firmly ahead of the other and walk away from your self-absorption. When you find the brighter-side of the Two garden, tap into your essential Four qualities of originality and creative expression. So, move out from under that weeping willow and wind your way home, perhaps discovering a rare wild yellow trout lily (dogtooth violet) along the path. Go ahead: dig it up, nobody's watching.

> *You know, one loves the sunset when one is so sad.*
> Antoine de Saint-Exupéry, *The Little Prince*

## How to Find Your Path "Home"

Oh, how the 4 Flower Gardener can *soar*, and the most fulfilling pursuit is to follow the carefully tended path to the Type 1 flower garden. When Type 4s recognize that they are already special—they find the light within rather than outside of themselves. And *wow*, that light shines! The 4 Gardener stops comparing herself to others and appreciates her unique gifts. When the Four is in "flow," she will literally skip to the 1 Flower Gardener, carrying a basket full of creativity and spontaneity! This path will require the Type 4 to venture by herself, and feel oh-so-special, and she can do it!

In the garden of the Type 1, the Four stops *talking* about her creative impulses and actually delivers the garden goods. In this 4/1 space, the Type 4 garden matures—and there is a true appreciation for all of the abundance.

## The Meaning of the Orchid Flower

Orchids are regarded as emblems of integrity, elegance, and friendship. Botanists agree that one feature above all others defines the orchid and differentiates it from virtually all other flowering plants: the fusion of the male and female portion into one structure. Unique indeed!

If the orchid is just too sophisticated for your taste, perhaps consider these other Four garden favorites (also see the Appendix):

**Sweet William**: Means *grant me one smile.*

**Columbine**: So unique—a reminder of deserted love.

**Bleeding Heart**: What a perfect 4-name—and this flower means to love unconditionally.

**Fuchsia**: Over 100 species in the evening primrose family—simply stunning.

## In Essence: Buttercup

Perhaps a distinctive scent to awaken the Type 4's senses is buttercup (let's use: *Ranunculus occidentalis*), which also can remind you of the beauty in the world. While the Four doesn't mind spending time in a "melancholy garden," she may need a little sniff to remind her to return to her radiant, inner light. Buttercup essence is known for its qualities to assist feelings of low self-worth and inability to experience one's inner light and uniqueness. This little boost will also help the 4 Gardener feel fulfilled in acts of service by not expecting anything in return.

So, my exquisite Four, when "in the doldrums" and you've had enough—find yourself a buttercup.

## Distinctive Hues of the Four Flower Gardener

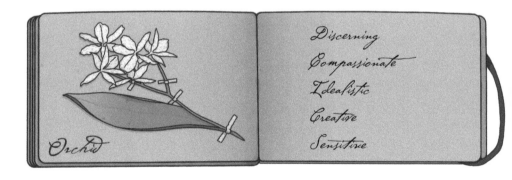

Orchid

Discerning
Compassionate
Idealistic
Creative
Sensitive

**Tips for the Type Four Gardener**

- Remember, ordinary can be beautiful too.
- Keep it simple but significant.
- Don't make your garden a crisis center.
- Listen to other gardeners' successes—smell their roses.
- Keep an eye out for garden-envy vine—it's invasive.
- Don't give up on your gardening gifts.
- Focus on what is in bloom, rather than what is missing.
- Nurture an unconditional garden—and apply that to friendships.

*Picking flowers in your garden*
*is like living in a rainbow.*
Kathleen Hunter

AND THE DAY CAME WHEN
THE RISK TO REMAIN IN A TIGHT BUD
WAS MORE PAINFUL THAN
THE RISK IT TOOK TO BLOSSOM.

ANAÏS NIN

## 5. The Observant Gardener
### 🌱 Bloodroot

I WOULD WAGER that, of all of the nine Enneagram types, perhaps it is the Type 5 Flower Gardener that is in the most trusting relationship with her garden. Why is this? Because the Type 5 engages in a bond with the garden, pledging a thoughtful, nurturing, guiding hand as needed; desiring only solitude in return.

No co-dependency garden here. Instead, the garden and gardener live in a parallel, natural universe with one another. You will be in awe of the 5 Gardener's deliberate and calm garden demeanor. Her garden is her coveted space, and she may lose track of all else as she carefully transplants and cultivates her beds.

So, if invited to visit, tread softly and leave your walking stick at the gate—the garden of the Type 5 is a sacred space in which to meditate.

## The Enneagram Type 5
## Gardener Type Checklist

- I spend a lot of time reading about various flowers and cultivation techniques.
- I prefer to spend time in my garden alone.
- I enjoy stepping away from my garden to reflect and analyze what I have created.
- I almost always seek information and knowledge before planting new flowers.
- I am interested in garden courses and self-learning.
- I think of a garden as a naturally evolving puzzle, and I enjoy placing and removing pieces.
- I will share my garden knowledge with others with whom I have mutual respect.
- I handle garden crises by investigating and taking steps to remedy the problem.
- I consider myself to be an objective gardener.
- I am focused in the garden and can easily lose track of time—working umpteen hours.

If your response is *YES, YES, that's me*, you might identify as a Type 5 Gardener.

*If you have a garden and a library,*
*you have everything you need.*
Marcus Tullius Cicero

## The Blossoms: The Strengths of the Type 5 Gardener

### The Contemplative Curator

You heard tell of a special, secret garden but are told it is difficult to reach. You set out to find it, following the narrow path, through a valley, across a rocky stream, and up a steep hill. Upon reaching your destination, you find a rather plain, wooden fence with a gate and a latch—that is rather uninviting. You think that you must have taken a wrong turn, as there is nothing special here!

And then you enter the gate. Below you, as far as you can see, are level upon level of a Zen-like garden that you might describe as a "garden puzzle." In the landscape before you, there are plant mazes, labyrinths, and interlocking pathways. Welcome to the curated garden of the Type 5. The 5 Gardener is often described as non-intrusive and circumspect. In fact, if you want to get to know a Five, you will have to be patient, as the Five, not unlike the unfurling moonflower, will reveal herself slowly and deliberately. To get to know her, one must be patient and look beyond the garden gate. However, once you enter, there are endless depths of knowledge and insight to explore. The Five's contemplative garden is a place of calm, away from the frantic pace of life. So, now that you've arrived, observe quiet, please, and pull out a notebook—because you are going to want to linger in this skillfully designed garden for a long while.

Type Fives are all about seeking knowledge and their garden beds reflect their scholarly acumen. The 5 Flower Gardener will have her plants in just the right spot to receive the requisite morning sun or afternoon shade. Excellent researchers, our 5s know the unique aspects of their garden terrain like an Italian knows the difference between rigatoni and linguini! You can bet that a Five will know better than to plant butterfly bush (*Buddleia*) in shade—how very *elementary, Watson!* The 5 Gardener does her homework, and trust me, she gets straight A's. I dare say, the Five is the most likely valedictorian of the garden. In fact, if you have a garden crisis, phone the 5 Gardener hotline (1-800-WISEBUD).

However, be warned: the Type 5 may not answer on the first ring. She guards her time wisely and appreciates garden privacy. She is likely to have her "ringer" off and take calls only during specified times. You will have to wait your turn—and when the Five is good-and-ready, she will find you. And you best be at the ready with your notepad, because you will be getting a garden-schooling!

*It's not just its satiny sweetness that makes the bloodroot flower so irresistible: it's also its ephemeral nature. Breathe too heavily and the petals shatter, the moment gone.*
Ketzel Levine

## The Purposeful Plot

The garden acronym F.I.V.E.-I-D.I.G. stands for: **First I Verify Every**-thing before **I Decide I Grow** anything! If you shun the thought of a garden blueprint, haven't heard of a soil test, or must take a wild guess about sun exposure—you are *Not a Five*! The 5 Gardener stands on the real or virtual balcony to survey, plan, plot, measure, and re-configure every aspect of the garden; all *before* she actually digs a hole!

Remarkable, you say? A Type 5 might respond, "My dear chap, I cannot imagine planning a garden any other way!" So, if you are reading this section reflecting on the disorganized pile that was once your garden—then re-read the previous section and get in the queue for a callback from the WISEBUD hotline. Once again, a 5 Gardener to the rescue.

## The Calm Cultivator

The 5 Flower Gardener radiates calm. In fact, Type 5s are often so immersed in their thoughts or observations, other gardeners may want to *accidently* squirt them with the hose to make sure they are alive. Naughty gardeners! That said, 5 Gardeners have this amazing superpower to literally remove themselves from the heat-of-the-moment and observe any scene, including the garden, from a detached point of view. Consider the Five as a bit like a squirrel, perched on a leafy branch, calmly calculating the theft and re-burial of your tulips.

Now, a non-flower gardener might be thinking that a garden isn't a typical emergency hotspot. *Au contraire!* Many a gardener has been seized by sheer, utter panic in seeing brown spots on their prized roses, or little holes on their calla lily leaves from some yet un-named varmint (although my money's on a dastardly bunny rabbit). So, if there were such a thing as a garden SOS Swat Team, you can bet your last precious pitcher plant, it would be a team of 5 Flower Gardeners. Calm in a storm and in the garden, the Five will pull out a reference, or just silently ponder—before calmly suggesting you chill out and let them "take the tiller." And if you are a Type 5 reading this, I may have inadvertently discovered your new day job: Emergency Garden Technician! Get it? E*M*T, E*G*T?!! Oh please, if you are a 5 Gardener, you know exactly what I'm talkin' about.

## THE WEEDS: THE CHALLENGES
## FOR THE TYPE 5 GARDENER

The wise 5 Flower Gardener is fully engrossed in planning, learning, and re-configuring a serene and thoughtful flower garden. In the garden of the Type 5, you are likely to find Zen-like Japanese maples and a variety of cacti. Why cacti, you ask? Because, the Five is much happier with a reality that will take care of itself. In this way, the 5 Gardener can remain more fully in the observer role—or in mind of the garden, so to speak—not so much amid the messy upkeep and constant care that needy-weedy flowers require.

Alas, just when tranquility descends, along come the new neighbors with their noisy lawn mower and "visiting" cat! Yes, regretfully, the world eventually seems to invade the 5 Gardener space. The Type 5 has some definite challenges—let's take a peek at a few Five foibles through the tiny hole in their garden gate.

### RECLUSIVE RHIZOME

Come out, come out, wherever you are! Remember that childhood game? You don't? Then you aren't as old as dirt, like the author of this book! Anyhoo, I digress. Being around a Type 5 is kind of like playing a game of hide and seek—except the 5 Gardener is usually hiding and really does not want to be sought or found! The Type Five in life, love, and in the flower garden can get a bad rap for seeming to be overly-detached, cold, and reclusive. Yikes—little garden-hermits, our 5s. In reality, the 5 Gardener is really not *cold* (okay, maybe chilly) but is afraid of experiencing the feelings that we all have. Instead of plunging headfirst into life and the messy stuff of humans, the Type 5 is actually quite content to hang out with her so-called *seedy* flower-buds. This can pose a bit of a problem, though, as to live life fully means to interact and share with (at least a few) other humans, not just the bees and butterflies. So please, gentle, wise 5 Gardener, climb down from your treehouse and join me on the garden swing. I promise not to take up too much of your time.

> *Flowers are the music of the ground.*
> *From earth's lips spoken without sound.*
> Edwin Curran

HOARDING HORTICULTURIST

Decisions over sunflowers (they cast shade over *everything*) or larkspur (they re-seed *everywhere*) or foxgloves (they bloom *every other* year)— ah, the joys of community flower gardening! And just when you need an answer to your communal quandary, the Type 5 goes underground like a mole in a Dutch tulip garden, with all of the tulip bulbs! Yep, the Five can get stingy with the facts and be unwilling to consider others' ideas—even if they are "sometimes" worth hearing! The 5 Gardener might be the proverbial gardener thinking *inside of* the garden box. What the Five doesn't realize is that sharing her inner world will truly help her reap what she sows. When the 5 Gardener shares, we are all so much better for it.

## Stuck in the Mud

The 5 Flower Gardener loves nothing more than amassing knowledge; however, she can struggle with needing more and More and MORE, until she is certain she has all of the facts. So, while not a *stick-in-the-mud*, the Type 5 does have a tendency to get a bit *stuck* in the mud. As any gardener knows, it is next to impossible to know everything about gardening, and as soon as one does, nature will always throw in a curveball. (Ever heard of *Fall Army Worms*? Neither had I, until they ate my front yard.) So, the wise Five falls into a trap and may not be able to move forward for fear of making a mistake or appearing uninformed. A stalled gardener is in a bit of a pickle, reading in the corner patch of soil. The risk here is that the 5 Gardener becomes a perennial garden *planner* and never a true, dirt-under-your-nails, gardener.

## Knowing When the Type 5 Is in the Brambles (Turn Back!)

The Five's experience of the world is basically that it is intrusive; however, when intrusive morphs to overwhelming and absolutely draining, the 5 Gardener will head down the path in the direction of the arrow and possibly draw from the less resourceful qualities of Type 7. This is really a bummer for those of us who count on the Five's calm and unflustered demeanor. Instead, we experience a disorganized, distracted 5 Gardener who seems unable to focus on the most basic of tasks, in the garden or life. On this side of the 5/7 space, the Five can become more than a wee-bit condescending and actually lapses into a hoarding over-drive—so hang on to your hostas, because the Type 5 won't be sharing anytime soon. We can only hope that the Five will wisely stroll to the adventurous side of a Type 7 garden to sow their knowledge and see it transformed into fascinating garden ideas and pleasurable, novel garden experiences.

*Gardening is learning, learning, learning.*
*That's the fun of them. You're always learning.*
Helen Mirren

## How to Find Your Path "Home"

The Type 5 Gardener is in high clover, and when she is feeling snug-as-a-bug, she might just be willing to emerge from her cocoon to venture on the path against the direction of the arrow to embrace the resourceful characteristics of the Type 8. Like Harry Potter's *Disapparate Spell*, you will not believe what you see—as the Five will metamorphose before your very eyes! Suddenly, the chill, Zen-like Five steps onto the main stage, sharing her wisdom magnanimously. This is huge, a garden analogy akin to a winter cyclamen morphing into a hot-pink summer dahlia! This is the 5/8 Flower Gardener that jumps off the balcony into the center of the garden stage, and in bold style picks a huge bouquet of whatever flowers she likes! No thought, no worry, just pure gut-like-Eight abundance. The Five goes Big before going home! You go, Type 5! You Go! We will all be cheering you on!

## The Meaning of the Bloodroot Flower

The bloodroot flower has several meanings, including protective love, purification, healing, as well as strength and growth. As a gift, these blooms can be given to represent a wish for the recipient to get well after an illness, to tell them they are loved, or simply to wish them the best for their life.

If the bloodroot flower is a bit too ephemeral (fleeting) for you, perhaps consider these other Five Gardener favorites (also see the Appendix):

**Cactus**: Symbolizes endurance and strength to survive in tough situations; as calm as can be—and thorny.

**Sea Holly**: Austere, purple beauty; fine to stand alone.

**Salvia**: Oh-so-wise, and the scent makes me feel smart.

**Hearts-a-Bustin'**: Named for the plant's unique four-lobed capsules that "bust" open to reveal bright-red seed hearts.

> *Give me odorous at sunrise a garden of beautiful flowers*
> *where I can walk undisturbed.*
> Walt Whitman

## In Essence: Cassiope

Remember reading about flower essences in Chapter 1? No? I can bet you remember if you are a Five. You not only read that section, but you Googled "The Science Behind Flower Essences" (every solid 5 Flower Gardener does a background check) and perhaps ordered a book on the so-called science behind essences. Now you can teach everyone else! Ah, this is why I love my 5 Gardener friends and colleagues: they study up while I'm arranging and delivering flower bouquets! Yay!

Back to what helpful blossom will nudge a heady Five to a feeling Five: How about a whiff of cassiope essence to quiet the ever-so-busy Type 5 mind. Cassiope is believed to induce a sense of warmth and joy for the physical body, replacing an imbalance toward the colder forces of intellect or technology. In a "positive cassiope state" (sounds like a song by a '60s rock band), the 5 Gardener will experience renewed joy for all human creation. So, perhaps if we are quiet we will even hear the cassiope softly humming "Here Comes the Sun," while the 5 Gardener turns toward the path of true harmony in mind-body-spirit.

*I'd like to be the kind of person who can enjoy things at the time, instead of having to go back in my head and enjoy them.*
David Foster Wallace

## DISTINCTIVE HUES OF THE FIVE FLOWER GARDENER

Observant
Detached
Deliberate
Discerning
Informed
Bloodroot

## Tips for the Type Five Gardener

- Do one spontaneous action in your garden every week.
- Find a time and place to explore creativity in your garden and life.
- Share your garden knowledge daily with other Flower Gardener friends and family.
- Move (literally!) from the planning stage to the doing stage.
- Allow yourself to experience feelings in the moment, and then let them go.
- Truly wise gardeners don't have the answer to everything.
- Enjoy inviting a friend to spend time with you in your garden.
- Buy some garden-luxury item for yourself and use it.

HELP US TO BE EVER FAITHFUL GARDENERS
OF THE SPIRIT, WHO KNOW THAT WITHOUT
DARKNESS NOTHING COMES TO BIRTH, AND
WITHOUT LIGHT NOTHING FLOWERS.
MAY SARTON

## 6. The Cautious Gardener
### ❧ Lavender

"THE SKY IS falling—run for cover!" says Chicken Little. "And a Hurricane is approaching!" replies the Six Flower Gardener! Even though, in reality, the approaching hurricane's name is Pee Wee, and it's a small storm off a coast far, far away!

Holy gladioli, if only Type 6s could let their field of fears lie fallow and enjoy the wildflowers. Six Gardeners are cautious and prepared to the nth degree, perched in the canopy of the tree, outfitted with binoculars in order to spot any approaching garden perils. The Paul Revere of the garden, our Type 6s, they will then swiftly announce, "The June Bugs are Coming! The June Bugs are Coming!" to all of their neighboring flower gardeners!

*Faith consists in believing when it is*
*beyond the power of reason to believe.*
Voltaire

# The Enneagram Type 6
## Gardener Type Checklist

- I often think of what can go wrong in my garden.
- I watch the weather and have concerns about droughts and flooding.
- I find myself questioning so-called garden experts.
- I tend to employ both wit and wisdom in my garden.
- I almost always second-guess my garden decisions.
- Being prepared is the basis for a lot of my life and garden decisions.
- I have a tendency to see the garden as half-empty.
- I like an orderly garden.
- When I hear *new and improved*, I tend to be skeptical.
- A beautiful flower garden is more about preparation than perspiration.

If your response is *YES, YES, that's me*, you might identify as a Type 6 Gardener.

## The Blossoms: The Strengths of the Type 6 Gardener

### The Cautious/Critical-thinking Cultivator

The 6 Flower Gardener is a cautious, crafty cultivator. While your gut-type gardeners may grab the shears and, like a brave knight, set out to slay the unwieldy *lorapetulum* shrub mid-summer, not so for the "thinking types"! The Type 6 plans first, then prunes. Smart move. (Note to non-Sixes: never, ever prune a flowering shrub mid-bloom!) So, when the garden mulch-chips are down, trust a 6 Gardener to make the right move and save the day (and perhaps your prize perennial).

We can all learn a lot from the Type 6. There is much garden-wisdom in proceeding with caution. The acronym W.A.I.T.—*Why Am I Trimming?*—was contrived by a 6 Flower Gardener, for sure. She will not only W.A.I.T., but you can count on her to ask the difficult, and perhaps, unpopular questions:

To a new homeowner wanting to plant oodles of spring bulbs, the Type 6 Gardener will ask, "Do you know what bulbs were previously planted in this bed? Perhaps wait and see—and plant your bulbs next spring?" (Other, not-6 Gardener: "But I want flowers *now!*")

To a random gardener wanting that beautiful, purple flower, wisteria, on their shed, the Type 6 will ask, "Do you know that wisteria, while very beautiful, will not only flower, it will pull down your whole shed?"

So, while that darn Six may seem to be procrastinating and voicing concerns, when you cannot wait to begin your next garden venture, my advice would be to listen up and perhaps heed her warnings. The Six will ask the tough questions and perhaps save you a future garden do-over.


## THE PROTECTIVE GARDEN BED

The 6 Flower Gardener is the one with the ergonomic gloves, sunscreen shirt, and lavender bug spray in her garden backpack. She will not only protect herself, but she is at the ready to protect her plants too. In the garden of the Type 6, all of the tender perennials and frost-avoidant flowers can rest easy, because the Six will make sure they are tucked in for the winter—whether with an extra-thick layer of mulch or in a cozy greenhouse.

Where *other* gardeners might say, *tough it out* (ahem: Type 8), the Type 6 is ready with a plant remedy and protective potion for leaf spots, over-watering, or not-so-friendly garden pests. A Six is reliable to those in her sphere in life and the garden. A Type 6 Gardener will protect you to the ends of the earth—or at least, till the end of the garden row. You aren't ploughing solo with a Six in your garden.

## The Witty Wildflower

It will not come as a surprise to those who know the "intellect types" (5s, 6s, and 7s), that they have quite the witty side in life, love, work, and garden. In particular, the 6 Flower Gardener often has a sense of her audience, enough to know what will bring on a good laugh. Perhaps this tendency is a snub to authority or to simply cope with her fears—but don't be surprised to see it manifested in the garden. Witty sculptures or birdhouse art, paths to nowhere or whimsical signs will often be found in the Six flower garden. I recall a Type 6 garden with a beautiful meditative labyrinth and a sign at the entrance—*Beware of Snakes*. Ah, I chuckled and thought, *my witty friend*—and then I warily STOMPED my way through my meditation. One can never be too cautious, right?

## The Loyal Leaf

Sixes in life and the garden are loyal and will stand-by-their-flowers through thick and thin. In flower-language, that means through droughts and floods, cold-snaps and heat-waves. As mentioned in the previous Blossoms section, this includes the Type 6 strategizing how to be most protective and planful, so as not to let her "buds" down. And when other gardeners may call it a day or night, the 6 Gardener will be working and re-thinking any lapses in judgment or reprimanding herself if she missed the smallest of details that led to the demise of one of her precious petaled friends. So, while 6 Gardeners may envision catastrophe and live with a constant degree of anxiety, they will come out a-fighting for you and their plants in the end. A steadfast and committed friend here.

> *But the calm had brought a sort of courage and hope with it.*
> *Instead of giving way to thoughts of the worst, he actually*
> *found he was trying to believe in better things.*
> Frances Hodgson Burnett, *The Secret Garden*

# THE WEEDS: THE CHALLENGES FOR THE TYPE 6 GARDENER

## THE CATASTROPHIC CULTIVATOR

Like Chicken Little, Sixes in life and in the garden are constantly on the look-out for the next catastrophe. The Type 6 envisions giant snails devouring their hostas and furtive rabbits just waiting their turn to nibble their toad lily leaves to the stem. Ever watchful and imagining every possible disaster is Type 6's way of maintaining a sense of control in an unpredictable garden landscape.

Just check out a 6 Gardener's shed—I'll guarantee you will find products ranging from Organic Rabbit-Be-Gone Spray to Fungicide-For-Everything from rust to aphids. The 6 Flower Gardener is prepared! I suspect a Six somewhere must have written *The Garden Disaster Handbook: How to Be Prepared, from Agitated Ants to Zombie Worms*. However, because of this very quality, a Six may be the most dependable of the nine Types. They will be at the ready with a back-up hosta when the deer eats yours the day before the annual garden tour. They are the literal garden-twine that holds up the trellis and allows our Carolina jasmine to climb ever higher. We are so very thankful to our 6 Gardeners, while we gently suggest that they *chill out*!

The Type 6 Gardener can't put her fears to rest and will literally wake up at night, slip on her garden boots, and put protective deer netting on her camellias by the light of the moon. You see, the Six is having a waking nightmare of the deer having a camellia midnight snack. The unpredictability of the garden and nature can be a bit unnerving for the orderly and fretful 6 Gardener. Once the "garden disaster" train leaves the station, the Type 6 can't get it to slow down. And as it picks up speed, there is not a single person on the planet that can out-fret a Six (except another Six). She handles her anxiety with careful planning, order, and choices. However, due to her rising fears of impending flower-doom, the 6 Gardener has trouble relaxing and relishing the blossoms.

## THE ANALYSIS-PARALYSIS PLANTER

The 6 Flower Gardener is full of doubts and questions, which can definitely be an issue in the garden. Just when the Six announces that she is going to go with coral azaleas at the front of her house, she begins to worry and doesn't trust her own decision. Thus begins the *Six Flower Gardener Garden-Quiz Show*! She will question everyone within earshot, including friends, family, the FedEx driver, the casual (perplexed) jogger who runs by: "Do you think azaleas will thrive in this spot? Should I go with coral or perhaps white? Quart size? Enough sun?" She will waffle and wonder until, alas, it is mid-summer, so she will now have to wait until fall.

This "makes for crazy" for all who know the 6 Gardener! You see, the problem is that Type 6s actually see both sides (and definitely downsides) of just about everything—and that leads to their indecision. The coral azaleas would be lovely, but the deer enjoy them as a noonday snack. Camellias, on the other hand, come in gorgeous shades of red, and the deer don't enjoy 'em. Oh, deer! Such decisions! The 6 Gardener is prone to perpetually retracing her steps and rethinking her choices. If I could take the liberty of re-writing a 6 Flower Gardener version of the famous poem by Robert Frost, "The Road Not Taken," it might read:

> *Two roads diverged in a wood,*
> *and I sat down for several days*
> *and thought about every darn peril possible,*
> *depending on which road I chose.*
> *And I—I'm still not totally sure I took the correct road,*
> *and that could make all the difference.*
> Type 6 Version of "The Road Not Taken"

## KNOWING WHEN THE TYPE 6 IS IN THE BRAMBLES (TURN BACK!)

Oh my, your anxious mind has taken over like an invasive mint, and you can't make enough mojitos to keep up with the supply. The Six Flower Gardener's tendency to see the world and garden through disaster-tinted shades can most definitely spell trouble. No matter which way they turn, the flower garden of the Type 6 becomes suspect! The Six is suspicious: Is that four-o'clock blooming late on purpose? Is that brugmansia betraying me by waiting to bloom until the day *after* the fall frost? No matter how many purple phlox are blooming, a little voice whispers, *the leaf mold is coming.* If only the 6 Gardener could stop tornado-ing herself into a twister, and chill out. Perhaps it would help to keep a magnet on the fridge that reassures, "Your Garden Is Committed to You—All Will Be Well!" And a second magnet that reads, "TRUST—Do Not Second-Guess the First Magnet!"

I propose to the Type 6: Dig a hole and bury those fears! Consider leaning on your Type 5 wing to prop up that falling sky. When the Type Six leans on her Five wing, she can perhaps fly solo and gain a broader perspective on what is feeding her anxiety. Or perhaps the 6 Gardener can sidle up to her 7 Gardener wing, where somewhere over the rainbow bluebirds fly, and there is a basket waiting, full of well-behaved, non-invasive mint plants! When leaning on her wing, the 7 Flower Gardener, the Six can delight and surprise us with animated adventure; albeit, with a backup plan lest the adventure turn into a disaster!

When garden plagues abound and the Six loses control, beware of turning in the direction of the arrow on the path to the less resourceful, *weedy* side of the Type 3 garden. This 6/3 path is unfortunately full of traps, and the Six will work ever-so-hard to maintain an image of competency, filling her garden shed with mounds of products and potions to control every possible pestilence. A trap indeed, as this route will not help the 6 Gardener gain the self-confidence she so desperately needs and deserves. We can only hope that in this space, the Six can stretch across to the deliberately planted rows of the Type 3's garden. In these 6/3 beds, she must nibble on the petals that provide her with the self-assurance that she is her own garden expert.

## How to Find Your Path "Home"

When the 6 Flower Gardener lets her worries run amuck, the best course of action is to try to take a healthier path away from the doubt and fear. On that route, she can perhaps forget about the sky falling—or think like a 7 Gardener and build a sun garden, 'cause it is gonna get awfully hot when that sky falls!

How fortunate that, when Type 6s are feeling more secure, they meander their way against the direction of the arrow to the all-is-well garden of the Type 9. In this 6/9 garden space, the Six is able to settle down, stop planning for catastrophes, and accept that there are many angles to her garden. This 6/9 combo allows the Type 6 to trust her garden-gut and become less reliant on the tomes of experts. She experiences empathy for herself and others, and you might even catch her humming with Bob Marley, "Every Little Thing Gonna Be Alright."

> *I go to nature to be soothed and healed,*
> *and to have my senses put in order.*
> John Burroughs

## The Meaning of Lavender

Lavender has been valued for centuries for its physical beauty, soothing fragrance, and healing properties. In addition, lavender flowers possess a unique meaning resonant to the 6 Gardener that translates as, "You have to be careful!"

If lavender leaves you a bit too calm, though, perhaps consider these other Type 6 garden favorites (also see the Appendix):

**Begonia**: Be cautious and think deeply.

**Datura**: Because every true Six needs some poison in the garden!

**Spiderwort**: Sounds scary but means truly loyal with high admiration.

**Iris**: Because "ya gotta have faith."

## In Essence: Cerato

Garden nightmares? It may sound like an oxymoron to most types, but not to the 6 Flower Gardener! Ever see the movie, *Little Shop of Horrors*? So, if you go to sleep dreading the next feature of *Poison Ivy Perils*, perhaps try a little essence whiff for renewed confidence upon waking. For the Six, the essence of the cerato flower might also guarantee sweet dreams. Cerato's positive qualities include trusting one's inner knowing and bolstering intuition, self-confidence, and certainty. A sniff of this true-blue flower will dispel the 6 Gardener's doubt of her inner wisdom and validate what she does know!

## Distinctive Hues of the Six Flower Gardener

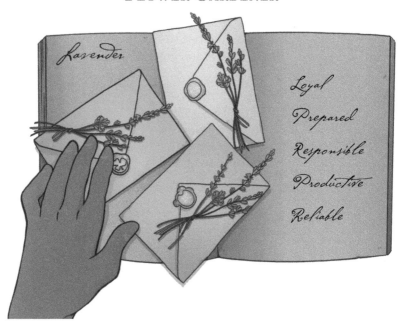

## Tips for the Type Six Gardener

- Trust your inner garden-gut guidance.
- Keep a journal of garden decisions that led to success.
- Note when you are acting like a pile of wet mulch, and see the positive side as well.
- Limit your web searches related to garden pests (or similar catastrophic topics).
- Try to distinguish between true garden disasters and free-range anxiety.
- Meditate daily in your garden to quiet your anxious mind.
- Practice not second-guessing the garden praise you receive.
- Hum the aforementioned Bob Marley tune as your garden theme song.

# 7. The Adventurous Gardener
## ❧ Clematis

WHILE THE TYPE 6 Flower Gardener is building her storm shelter and battening down the hatches, the Type 7 Gardener is imagining a beautiful garden canal filling with water—and doodling the details of her crystal rowboat in which she will ride out the storm. After the rains, she envisions herself floating among the lily pads above the koi. Our Type 7 is weary of her neighboring 6 Wing's ruminations full of dark clouds and fierce winds.

Type 7 Flower Gardeners have lush landscapes in their minds, in such detail, that only a Seven could dream them up. Their creative, mental energy fuels them to such a degree that I am certain that the word *imagine* was coined by a Type 7.

*There is nothing like a dream*
*to create the future.*
Victor Hugo

# The Enneagram Type 7
## Gardener Type Checklist

- My garden is always coming up roses.
- Anticipating and planning my spring garden is the best part of gardening.
- I love a variety of flowers in my garden and appreciate spontaneous blossoms.
- When a pest destroys plants in my garden, I look on the bright side and move on.
- I get bored with the routine tasks of gardening.
- A garden is meant to be a joyful, happy place, not drudgery and weeding.
- I think some gardeners take their flowers and plots way too seriously.
- I'd much rather start something in my garden than finish it—I'm on to the next idea.
- Variety, spontaneity, and fun are the only ways to garden.
- A day spent at farmers' markets and garden shops is my kind of day.

If your response is *YES, YES, that's me*, you might identify as a Type Seven Gardener.

> *The flower that follows the sun*
> *does so even in cloudy days.*
> Robert Leighton

## The Blossoms: The Strengths of the Type 7 Gardener

### Enthusiastic Euphorbia

The Type 7 comes by her description honestly. She is adventurous, enthusiastic, and full of ideas. While the Type 6 is bemoaning a myriad of garden perils, the 7 Gardener is visualizing an equal measure of floral delights. The enthusiastic Seven is imaginative and adventurous, so just beware—if you idly mention a seemingly wild and zany garden concept, the 7 Flower Gardener will quite possibly call your bluff and double down with three more equally outrageous ideas! So, if you are weary of garden worry and woe—put down your hoe and make your way to the Type 7 garden, where the sun is perpetually shining and gentle breezes blow.

## THE BOUNTIFUL GARDEN BED

Picture, if you will, a 7 Flower Gardener, throwing a handful of wild-flower seeds and anticipating what might germinate in the early spring. That imagined garden in the 7's mind is so much more fun than the reality of the few, straggly cosmos, zinnias, and cleome that actually germinate. (Note to all Flower Gardeners: stop buying packets of wildflower seeds in the hope of a garden looking like the slopes of Aspen during spring. Not happening. Just not.) But the Type 7 is actually fine if the result isn't what she hoped for, because by the time spring arrives, she is on to several other garden projects and imagining new adventures.

When it comes to the mundane tasks of tilling, pruning, and harvesting, the Type 7 might suddenly be up-up-and-away, perhaps in a hot-air balloon, on a mini-vacation, or involved in some cool new hobby. Your 7 Gardener friend will express that she is oh-so-sorry, and will be there *next time*. Hmm, one can only wish the Seven *Bon Voyage*!

In the midst of winter, with ice on the trees and no end to frigid temperatures, most gardeners fall into what is termed, *depression*! But the 7 Flower Gardener is in her very own imaginative garden heaven. I once read that for the Type 7, it is *in the waiting, not the sating*, that provides her with enough brain-candy to last through the cold, long winter. While the rest of us realists are waiting out the winter storms, the Seven has surrounded herself with garden catalogs, highlighter in hand! The 7 Flower Gardener in running on natural adrenaline, no fertilizer necessary.

The long winter, though, is just long enough to get the Type 7 into some serious trouble—perhaps over-ordering (did she click on five ruby re-blooming azaleas or fifteen?) and thus adding new plans for a garden pond with three tiers. A 7 Flower Gardener, unchecked, will perhaps get in way over her head, and who will help do the digging, planting, mulching? Not a Seven—boring, boring. Time to phone her Type 1 BFF— she'll do some heavy lifting because (as any 1 Flower Gardener will tell you) it's the right thing to do!

To the Seven there is an upside to almost anything—one just has to re-imagine and create a positive story! No sad ending to this garden tale, only happy trails!

### LIGHTHEARTED

The honeysuckle is enveloping the front door, the mailbox is smothered in Carolina jasmine, and the brugmansia towers over the roof! It's August in the Type 7's flower garden—call it, Garden-Gone-Wild—and the Seven is having a ball! If she had just one message to share with the rest of us, it would be, "Lighten up, will ya?" The 7 Flower Gardener believes that life is short, the summer days are long, and there is no use in spending all of your time and energy perfecting, achieving, perseverating, and worrying when you can, PLAY!

Of the Enneagram types, the Type 7 has the most childlike response to the garden, truly appreciating the smells and textures. To that end, you might catch a 7 Flower Gardener blowing a dandelion flower to send its seeds shimmering in the air, or nuzzling her face against the soft, fuzzy petals of the flowering purple *Tibouchina*. These experiences speak to the Seven's vivacity and colorful nature. Her optimism suggests we should all pay attention to the proverb, "All work and no play makes Jack a dull boy"—and perhaps, Jill a dull girl!

Of course, subsequent writers (clearly not Type 7s) have suggested, "All play and no work makes Jack a mere toy"—and this phrase, regretfully, leads us into the 7 Flower Gardener weeds. My apologies to all my fun-loving Seven friends that we must venture into the weeds for a wee-while; perhaps the following quote will help ease the transitional pain.

*If you feel lost, disappointed, hesitant, or weak,*
*return to yourself, to who you are, here and now*
*and when you get there, you will discover yourself, like a lotus*
*flower in full bloom, even in a muddy pond, beautiful and strong.*
Masaru Emoto

## The Weeds: The Challenges for the Type 7 Gardener

In the 7 Flower Gardener's pursuit of being in a world of possibilities and adventures, she may find she has wandered outside of her garden and into the woods and brambles with no breadcrumb trail to get home. Where before, the sky was the limit, in this space the Seven begins to feel claustrophobic. Having strayed afar, the Type 7 may become demoralized, pessimistic, and judgmental—a self-appointed garden-monitor and critic. Let's explore a few of the cuts and scratches of the challenged 7 Gardener, and then move forward to pathways out of the thorny woods!

### Greener Grass?

An apt title for the Seven may be the garden *epicure*, as she wants to have her roses, smell them too, and frankly, would prefer them to be of many varieties. Our Type 7 is a bit "sameness" phobic—so she will plant her garden with an eye to changing it up when she tires of the same ol' blooms. Don't be surprised if you go to visit your Seven friend and you find she has completely upended her perennial bed to create a Zen garden after her recent trip to Japan. Dare you remind her just how much she spent on the perennials she just tore out and replaced with bonsai? What another Type might suggest as tried-and-true or tradition, a 7 Flower Gardener might view as tedious and tiresome.

Type 7s envision greener pastures, in life and in their gardens. I once heard tell of a 7 Gardener who, bored with her cereal and banana breakfast, began to invite the deer in each day for an evergreen-hosta buffet! Seriously. Call me crazy, but I prefer a solitary reading of *The New York Times* with my first cup of coffee. Enter the world of a Seven, and proceed with caution as you literally can't imagine what lies ahead.

### Gobs of Garden

Our Type 7 gardening friends delight in new adventures and possibilities in life and in their gardens. As one introverted 7 Flower Gardener stated,

"Looking at all the possible flowers I can buy is like brain candy—I just can't stop thinking about all of the options!" No wonder the Enneagram passion of the Type 7 is "gluttony," or in this case, garden-gluttony! So much to fantasize about, so much to buy! "In with the new _____ (insert new varietal) and out with the old _____ (insert boring plant name)" could be their motto. If you want to witness 7 Gardener euphoria, ask her to join you at a premier botanical garden. I'm thinking of Butchart Gardens in British Columbia, Canada. This world-renowned garden is like a gigantic garden tapas plate! The only problem is that she will be so mesmerized by the varieties of plants she may try to hide under a giant fern and stay for the night. Typical Type 7: boundless joy and endless curiosity!

### The Pest Avoidant Planter

The song of the 7 Flower Gardener might be, "Don't Rain on My Parade," from the musical, *Funny Girl*. A soft rain in their garden is one thing, but not when they are ready to host their garden party! The bottom line is that 7 Flower Gardeners don't want to be tied down, nor do they want to be bored!

That said, when the going gets tough, the Seven just might get going! I know it might appear that I'm being tough on Type 7s, but the truth is that 7 Gardeners, in general, prefer the fun, the adventure, and the dream versus, well, the tiresome and boring reality. So when the weeds are tall and annoying, the toad lily has "rust" on its leaves, and a squirrel has dug up the very last fall crocus—the Type 7 might decide to "get away" from the garden tedium. The get-away might be physical or mental. So many ideas; should the Seven spend the day digging into a juicy novel rather than the bone-dry soil? Bottom line, most 7 Flower Gardeners start singing a catchy tune, as they just want to hum away the sorrow. That's the truth, and I'm stickin' to it!

## Knowing When the Type 7 Is in the Brambles (Turn Back!)

So, while our 7 Flower Gardeners would love to live perpetually in the Land of Oz—alas, they sometimes take the wrong turn and find themselves off of the yellow brick road.

When the Type 7 follows the path in the direction of the arrow to the 1 Flower Gardener, they unfortunately, more often than not, move in a less-than-resourceful way. No rainbows and fairytales when this happens—instead, the adventurous, joyful Seven in colorful Oz moves to the world of black-and-white and takes on the judgmental and accusatory aspects of the Type 1. In this 7/1 garden, it seems that nothing *is coming up roses*, and all of the garden beds are coming up weeds.

Moreover, in this garden her gloves are pointing at "others." If you happen to cross garden paths with a 7 Flower Gardener when they've landed in this inauspicious space, you will experience a Jekyll-and-Hyde moment! You will wonder what strange magic is afoot that changed your usually fun-loving, inspirational friend into a hyper-critical perfectionist.

My advice is to take heart—and perhaps nudge your friend toward the resourceful side of the 1 Flower Gardener. In this realistic 7/1 garden, the ideas begin to come together with a focus and clear path to bring dreams to fruition. And as this 7/1 garden takes shape, you might gently guide the Type 7 Flower Gardener back to the sign for the yellow brick road. On the Enneagram, that would be on the path in the direction against the arrow to the resourceful Type 5 flower garden! Cut through the wildflower meadow and meet them there!

> *"Of course there must be lots of Magic in the world," he said wisely one day, "but people don't know what it is like or how to make it. Perhaps the beginning is just to say nice things are going to happen until you make them happen. I am going to try and experiment."*
>
> Frances Hodgson Burnett, *The Secret Garden*

## How to Find Your Path "Home"

Securely back on the yellow brick road, the 7 Flower Gardener avoids the Wizard of Oz's garden of smoke and mirrors, and instead, in the Five flower garden, the Type 7 transforms from flying sorcerer to grounded sage. In the 5 garden, Sevens recognize that perhaps more is, in fact, too much, and they begin to explore their own garden and life on a much deeper level. In the tranquility of the Five garden, Type 7 realizes that Oz, while beautiful, wasn't real, and she returns to her metaphorical Kansas—home—recognizing she can now face her fears head-on and find satisfaction in the here-and-now.

## The Meaning of the Clematis Flower

The actual term *clematis* means or relates to the world of mental beauty! What better flower to associate with our mentally adventurous 7 Flower Gardener! Much like the Seven, the clematis loves to travel, winding her way cleverly around twigs and trellises toward the sun to gain a new perch—blooming brightly along the way.

If the clematis is too high a climb, perhaps consider these other Seven Flower Gardener favorites (also see the Appendix):

**Poppy**: Imagination, oblivion, and pleasure.

**Marigold**: As happy as can be.

**Chrysanthemum**: Excitement and optimism.

**Calendula**: Folk name is "summer's bride," as the flower head turns as the summer sun moves through the sky.

> *Hello, sun in my face.*
> *Hello, you who made the morning*
> *and spread it over the fields ...*
> *Watch, now, how I start the day*
> *in happiness, in kindness.*
> Mary Oliver

## In Essence: Agrimony

The 7 Flower Gardener will literally want to sniff all of the essences, and would find nothing better than stopping and smelling the roses; well, the *stopping* might be hard—they would be whizzing by and smelling the roses and anticipating the next scent! So, what the Type 7 needs is a little sniff of agrimony to help them remain positive while being present for life's down times. Agrimony flower essence is known to help a person experience inner peace and harmony, while being emotionally honest. In a positive agrimony state, a person can process disharmonious life events while still remaining positive. Sounds like a win-win to me.

> *Life is not measured by the number of breaths you take, but by*
> *the moments that take your breath away.*
> Maya Angelou

## Tips for the Type Seven Gardener

- Practice a little restraint; more flowers do not necessarily equate to a more beautiful garden.
- Meditate. In your garden. Alone. That means quiet-mind time.
- When you feel garden frustrations and remain in that emotional state, applaud yourself—that is a sign of true growth.
- Don't start a new garden bed or project until the current one is complete.
- Try to stay present for others' frustrations and pain—in life and in the garden.
- When the garden gets tough, don't "get going." Stay. Dig. Sweat.
- Get out of your head and feel the earth.
- Gardening is a daily form of exercise. Just Do It.

IF YOU ASK ME WHAT
I CAME INTO THIS WORLD TO DO
I WILL TELL YOU, I CAME TO LIVE OUT LOUD.

ÉMILE ZOLA

## 8. The Self-reliant Gardener
### ❧ Black-eyed Susan

MY HUSBAND MARTY's favorite movie is the *original*, 1933 *King Kong* featuring Fay Wray as Ann Darrow. If you haven't seen it, hit the pause button right now, make yourself a big bowl of popcorn, and settle in for one of the great classics. So, "What does this have to do with flowers and the Enneagram?" you ask. Fair question, and I'll ask you to keep reading about the Type 8 (protective, self-reliant, competitive). Although I have no actual proof, I am 99.9% certain that the seemingly invincible Kong, the King of the Jungle, was a Type 8 (God rest his big soul). And I am quite sure that my husband identifies with that gorilla, because he is Type 8 as well! But here is the reason I am sure that King Kong was a Type 8: underneath his huge, blustering presence and fierce roar, he had a tender, loving heart. After all (spoiler alert!), *It was beauty killed the beast*. Now let's enter the garden jungle of the Type 8 Flower Gardener!

# The Enneagram Type 8
## Gardener Type Checklist

- I'm wary of people or plants that are too well behaved.

- I don't have much respect for people or plants that don't stand up for themselves.

- I don't like it when people beat around the flower bush—I prefer direct communication.

- I make garden decisions fast, based on my instinctive garden-gut.

- I like a garden that can take care of itself during droughts and freezes.

- I don't mind arguing with the community garden club committee.

- Under my tough, garden skin I have a *bleeding heart*.

- When I'm in my garden, I take care of what needs to be done before frivolities.

- Don't mess with me, people I love, or my garden (that includes you, "deer"!).

If your response is *YES, YES, that's me*, you might identify as an Eight Flower Gardener.

*She made herself stronger*
*by fighting with the wind.*

Frances Hodgson Burnett,
*The Secret Garden*

## The Blossoms: The Strengths
## of the Type 8 Gardener

### Powerful Pruner

I'm still on King Kong, just for a little bit longer. If you have yet to watch the movie (*as I previously recommended*) then skip to the next section, "The Confident Cultivator."

So, in the movie, the men thought that KK was going to kill the beautiful actress, Ann Darrow (frankly, so did she, for a while), until she quickly realized that King Kong was the best chance she had for getting out of that God-forsaken jungle alive. That aptly describes the 8 Flower Gardener in a jungle, garden, or life: they will have your back through thick and thin. If you are gardening with a Type 8, she will combat fire ants, Japanese hornets (my dear Type-8 husband once donned a literal garden hazmat suit to go after a colony of these stingers), poison ivy, or venomous snakes. Just yell, "Help! Copperhead!" and any 8 Gardeners within hollering range will come a-running with their hoes.

To the Eight, gardening is not for the faint of heart. If there is a task to be done, she is all about it. However, do not waste her time. Do not ask a Type 8 to do some pansy-a_ _ job, because Eights comes in two flavors, Bold and Extra Bold. If you are up for the task, then just do it; and if not, get out of the way, 'cause the 8 Flower Gardener will protect you and save your gardening day.

### The Confident Cultivator

To utter the phrase *compete in a garden* is akin to suggesting *combat in yoga*: oxymoron! However, when it comes to the 8 Flower Gardener, all bets are off. Take, for example, the gentle, masterful team of horticulturists in the neighborhood community garden. The 8 Gardener merely wants to know who's at the head of the garden row, so to speak. That's all, no big deal, right? Wrong. Type 8s will have zero tolerance for a garden guru who doesn't lead with total confidence and a course of action. If the guru is ineffectual, the path may be strewn with dead-headed daisies, as the Eight will decidedly test the guru's authority.

The 8 Flower Gardener is in the community garden to *get it done*, not to waste time waffling between planting plumbago or verbena! Petal-up my friends, or the Type 8 will take the hoe and tend the row—preferably, solo! The garden insight here is that the 8 Gardener doesn't really want or need to be the person *in control*, she just doesn't want to *be* controlled—which makes living with and loving Type 8s an endlessly fascinating dance!

BOLD BOUQUET

I read a great description of the Type 8 in a book by Cron and Stabile, *The Road Back to You*. The line describes the Type 8's "deadly sin" (wow, that sounds horrible, but each Type gets their own) of *Lust*. It states that Eights "don't come equipped with dimmers"—they are On or Off, All In or All Out. Basically, this refers to the 8 Flower Gardener's desire for intensity, and the Type 8 motto might be, "Go Big or Go Home!"

In the garden, this often shows up when the 8 Flower Gardener opts for flowers with bold scents or colors. It can also manifest when she uses her new tree trimmer attachment to trim, not one, not two, but *every tree*! The Type 8 will then collapse for the evening, having gone full speed ahead with her new trimmer toy. So, the adage *Ready-Aim-Dig!* does not apply to the Eight in the garden—instead the 8 Flower Gardener lives by *Dig-Ready or Not*. And if the Type 8 has a rototiller, you best get out of the way! One might call this approach to life a bit excessive, but to 8 Flower Gardeners it's a routine expression of their fierce energy and appetite for life. I find it fascinating that, in general, a Type 8 has no clue that she presents an intense and forceful approach in her daily interactions. In fact, if I had a bulb for every time I shared this observation with an Eight, I'd have a field of tulips!

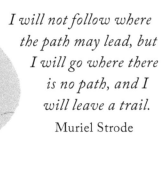

*I will not follow where
the path may lead, but
I will go where there
is no path, and I
will leave a trail.*
Muriel Strode

### INFLUENTIAL IRRIGATOR

Truth be told, Type 8s intimidate the heck out of the best of us and, frankly, some do it on purpose to basically weed out the weaklings. Call it a kind of "personality" soil test for the 8 Flower Gardener—as they test conditions to decide if they want to spend time with you in the garden of life. they make a decision of who will stay on "their team" and who will need to go, the Eight will wield their instinctual justice toward those for whom they have no respect, until those folks pick up their garden pails and are grateful to be dismissed from the greenhouse!

Of course, this is all part of the 8 Flower Gardener's plan to use her influence to create a just and equitable community. And while their decisions may or may not always be accurate, Type 8s will strive to be fair as they take justice into their own sturdily gloved garden hands. I must admit, as a routinely accommodating Type 2 Flower Gardener, I'm rather fascinated by the 8 Flower Gardener's enviable and charismatic flower-power!

# The Weeds: The Challenges for the Type 8 Gardener

## Badass Bed

No violets or weeping willows for our 8 Flower Gardeners— regardless of the flower, the name just won't do. The Type 8 in life and in the garden is strong and tough, and so are her plants. For example, during one North Carolina summer, when even the sunflowers in our garden were wilting, I told my husband we needed to install an irrigation system. I was done, *done*, with spoon watering each pitiful plant. His response was, basically, if they can't *tough out* an NC summer drought, they need not be in our garden. That's an Eight for you: if you can't make it, step out of the way (or clay, in this case) and move on to some tropical rainforest garden!

The Type 8 plants a garden that mimics her own personality, full of only tough, hardy plants, ready to survive an upstate NY winter or an NC drought. What the 8 Gardener is missing, however, is that in the garden and life, our vulnerability makes us stronger, not weaker. Perhaps for a lesson the Eight should look to the (believed-to-be vulnerable) pansy as it turns its velvety, yellow-purple head to the sun, despite harsh February winds and snow drifts. In fact, the gentle pansy has it within its genes to withstand the cold! The lesson: tenderness and strength can co-exist in the garden and in life.

## Argumentative Turf

Make no mistake, the 8 Flower Gardener can argue with an earthworm. I'm not joking. The earthworm will undoubtedly lose. A good verbal brawl gives the Type 8 a chance to remind all of us mere mortal flower gardeners that she is the real deal. So, if you are face-to-face with an 8 Gardener who senses an injustice, and you can't stand your garden-ground, I would advise you to pick up your bucket and trowel and just go home. You see, Eights get a honey-suckle high from an argument! They are in their element when standing up to the neighborhood jerk or the Home Garden Store clerk that sold them a bum brunnera or a crummy camellia. The garden gloves come *off*, and the spring shoppers will drop their daisies to enjoy the show! However, the Eight has forgotten the Proverb, *You can catch more flies with honey than vinegar*. And while she will feel justified in standing her ground in the moment, she has likely burned many a bridge along the way.

> *The quieter you become, the more you can hear.*
> Ram Dass


## (Not) Invincible-Terrain

You may have heard of Harry Potter's cloak of *invisibility*—when he dons it, he renders himself invisible to others as he stealthily makes his way around Hogwarts! Well, the 8 Flower Gardener dons a cloak of *invincibility*. The problem is that Type 8s never take their cloak off!

Eight Flower Gardeners have absolutely no idea what "everything in moderation" means. The Type 8 lives by the phrases, *All Out* and *It's All or Nothing*—and that spirit definitely shows up in the garden. Constraints be damned, whether digging up a tap-root that has reached China or eradicating English ivy that has engulfed fifteen acres of woodland. The 8 Gardener will wrangle that ivy like Hercules slaying the nine-headed Hydra, not stopping until the Ivy-Be-Conquered! The teensy-tiny issue here is that most Eights ain't Hercules (or KK)—they are quite mortal, and they might risk their health and safety in their belief that they are more powerful than mere mortal gardeners. If you are fortunate to have an 8 Flower Gardener in your life, you might be able to talk her out of the tree—and encourage her to come to earth, literally.

The message here is: please, lighten up, my non-invincible 8 Flower Gardener, and recognize that you might (just) get by with a little help from your friends. In reality, you will not only get by, but you'll survive and thrive.

*Anybody who wants to rule the world*
*should try to rule a garden first.*
Gardening Saying

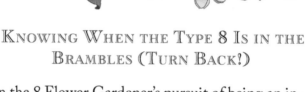

## KNOWING WHEN THE TYPE 8 IS IN THE BRAMBLES (TURN BACK!)

In the 8 Flower Gardener's pursuit of being an independent, protective gardener, she may find she has taken her *fee-fi-fo-fum* (recall the giant in *Jack and the Beanstalk*?) refrain a bit too far and ended up stomping down the path in the direction of the arrow to the un-resourceful side of the Type 5 garden. And instead of striking fear in the faint of heart, and compelling others to heed their wise, gut-wisdom and directives, the 8 Flower Gardener becomes disconnected with her emotions. Gone is the bold Eight that we know and love, and we are faced with a secretive, hypervigilant 8/5 combo, expecting betrayal and mistrust at every turn. The 8 Flower Gardener on this path can end up with lots of scrapes, as in this 8/5 garden she sees the world as "with me" or "against me," and ends up at an uncompromising "against me" dead end.

That's when we cross our fingers and hope that the Type 8 finds a healthy life-vine and pulls herself back up the beanstalk. In the high-side of the 5 garden, the 8 Gardener will find a balance between perspiration and observation, demonstrating some neutrality. In the 8/5 garden space, the type 8 begins to view herself as a person who gains plant wisdom and shares it magnanimously, learning the true power of shared knowledge.

## How to Find Your Path "Home"

One of my favorite phrases has always been, *between a rock and a heart space*, until I was told I actually had the wording wrong. The accurate phrase is *between a rock and a hard place*, i.e., making a choice between two unacceptable possibilities. (Frankly, I prefer my version!) But my take on this saying is the perfect quote for the 8 Flower Gardener to *dig deep*, let down her strong-rock façade, and trust that the resourceful path is to venture against the direction of the arrow toward the heart space of the 2 Gardener.

In this 8/2 garden, the invincible 8 Gardener gets in touch with her warm and giving nature. To be clear, to risk heading down this path, the Type 8 has to be convinced that she can *trust herself* with you. I implore you, if you find an 8 in this 8/2 flower garden, please don't let her down—and you will be rewarded with a bouquet of abundant flowers.

On a side (but important) note, the gifted author and speaker Brené Brown writes that when we are able to embrace love and belonging, we become vulnerable *and* brave. Here's to the Eight that ventures to this beautiful 8/2 Flower Gardener space, opening her compassionate heart while maintaining her strong backbone. We will meet you there, kind and strong 8 Flower Gardener!

## The Meaning of the Black-eyed Susan

The black-eyed Susan represents justice, which is the quality embraced by the 8 Flower Gardener. Also a symbol of motivation, the black-eyed Susan's bright yellow halo of blossoms surrounding the dark, inner core embodies protection and strength given to the solar plexus to release old habits and negative behaviors. Remember, the Type 8 is of the *Instinctive* or *Gut* triad.

If the black-eyed Susan flower is not bold enough for you, consider these other Eight Flower Gardener favorites (also see the Appendix):

**Camellia**: Strong desire and excellence, even when it is really cold outside.

**Foxglove**: Means insincerity, and Type 8s know it when they see it.

**Gladiolus**: They stand tall, personifying strength of character.

**Angel's Trumpet**: I feel emboldened when I catch a whiff of its strong scent.

## In Essence: Cherry Plum

Eight Flower Gardeners love a good, strong scent, so why not take a whiff of something that will yield big results? For the Type 8, that just might be cherry plum essence!

Even the most self-aware and resourceful Eights struggle with loss of control and keeping those big emotions in check. Welcome cherry plum essence to perhaps help you let go of past, regrettable behavior and stop worrying about repeating it in the future. Cherry plum boosts the calm control that the 8 Gardener needs and enhances patience and tolerance.

Hmm. Perhaps the Type 8 might share some of that essence with the rest of us!

High Energy
Confident
Autonomous
Competent
Hardworking

Black Eyed Susan

## Tips for the Type Eight Gardener

- Try moderation in one endeavor in life and the garden (you can do it, *just one*).
- All matters aren't black and white—look to your spring garden as an example.
- Reflect and prepare what you want to put in your garden before digging it up.
- Try not to intimidate other gardeners—it's a hobby, after all.
- When you begin to raise your voice at the Home and Garden Shop, take note and simmer down.
- Perhaps you were wrong about _____ (insert incorrect flower garden decision); just perhaps?
- Enjoy the tender vulnerability of the early spring garden, and know that tenderness is a gift.
- Embrace tiny perennials—not all flowers in your garden have to be big and bold.

My heart wants roots.
My mind wants wings.
I cannot bear their bickering.

E. Y. Harburg

# 9. The Peaceful Gardener
## 🌿 Windflower

WHILE THE NINE's wing, the 1 Flower Gardener, is all about getting their garden *right*, the 9 Gardener is all about gaining perspective. On Nine's *other* wing, the Type 8s are plotting, digging, and planting—while 9s might very well be taking a break in the hammock, considering a multitude of planting options. They have spent the long winter months perusing seed catalogs (so many options!) and are *almost* ready to place their order, but they want to check out *one more* website before making their final choices. The time and energy spent on making these choices is just draining, thus the need to rest a while in the hammock!

Perhaps the 9 Flower Gardener will finally place that order and put those seeds in the ground—or, there's always next spring! No worries, the Nine has plenty of other things to distract her; and besides, it's likely July by now!

## The Enneagram Type 9
## Gardener Type Checklist

- I can get lost in trivia instead of focusing on necessary garden chores.
- When the garden committee pressures me to change my mind, I *dig in* and get stubborn.
- I need a little push to get started on garden tasks—but once I get going, I get a lot done.
- I may appear more peaceful than I really am inside.
- Conflict—ugh! I prefer to choose the garden path of least resistance.
- I opt to use "zone out" strategies instead of dealing with life—like watching *The Princess Bride* for the tenth time.
- If I have garden partners, I am likely to go along with whatever *they* want to do.
- I'm fine to "make do" rather than "make perfect."
- I prefer quiet garden time to a garden party.
- It's difficult to make life and garden decisions.

If your response is *YES, YES, that's me,* you might identify as a Nine Flower Gardener.

*Part of the delight of my garden is that you just get lost in it before you've started to do anything.*
Ross Gay

## The Blossoms: The Strengths
## of the Type 9 Gardener

### The Empathetic Bed

You now know that you can have a good cry in the Type 4 garden, pick a bouquet in the Type 2's, and get your organic flower fungicides in the

6's. But if you need someone to just listen, to just about *anything*, take the garden path to the flower garden of the Type 9.

Not only will she put down the trowel—she will throw in the towel and pack up for the day. She will then ever-so-gently enter your garden space. The Nine will listen and empathize with whatever is grieving or peeving you, and you will feel as though she has all of the time in the world—and completely understands where you are coming from, or going to. Nine Gardeners are in the moment—and this one is about you. In fact, it is much easier for the Type 9 to listen to, worry about, and tend to your life/garden woes than to tend to her own! Thus the 9 Gardener settles in and feels the depth of your experience, merging with your angst or joy. Kind and compassionate listeners are our Nines. So plump up a clover pillow and nestle on that bed of mulch. The Type 9 Flower Gardeners are the true peacemakers of the planet we call Earth.

## DIGGING FOR DIPLOMACY

I still remember taking two of my garden buddies from the Midwest on the Charleston, South Carolina, annual Home and Garden Tour—a spectacular spring event that showcases gardens throughout the city. At each home garden, a small group tours with a Master Gardener Docent—who, true to Southern style, dons a large-brimmed, floppy hat and gently shares about the well-tended plant varieties. During our tour, the docent passed by a rather exotic looking flower, so my Midwestern friend (probably a Type 8 Flower Gardener) asked the docent if she could provide information on the plant. The docent, clearly not knowledgeable about the particular plant, stopped, smiled, and in a very beautiful Southern accent stated, "Well, let's put our heads together and try to figure out what that plant is." I still remember my 8 Flower Gardener friend's indignant expression at this (basically) *non*-response! However, looking back, I'll bet you my tulip bulbs that the docent was a Type 9 Gardener. The Type 9 in the garden and life is a diplomat to the nth degree. When she gets a whiff of conflict or dissent, she will strive to calm the waters. As with our docent, the Nine will seek the perspective of others and strive for a harmonious solution in all matters great and small.

## Take Your Flowering Thyme

Nine Flower Gardeners take the time to examine various pieces of garden information, using sources ranging from the *Farmer's Almanac* to the latest technological advances, and then weave them together like a beautiful grapevine wreath. The strength of the Type 9 is gaining perspective before rushing to action. While many a novice flower gardener, in her haste for spring blossoms, will mistakenly stick salvia in dense shade or a bleeding heart in full sun—this will not be the case for the thoughtful Nine. She will nestle herself in the garden hammock, preferably solo, and take her time to let her garden evolve. And after she has done her due-garden-diligence, she will set about purposefully placing bulbs and plants in her thoughtful garden beds. No haste-makes-waste label will ever be applied to a 9 Flower Gardener! She will definitely take her flowering-thyme, and the result will be spectacular.

> *I always see gardening as escape, as peace really.*
> *If you are angry or troubled, nothing provides*
> *the same solace as nurturing the soil.*
> Monty Don

## HARMONIOUS TERRAIN

The 9 Flower Gardener appears to be the most agreeable of all of the nine Enneagram Flower-Gardener Types. She will eagerly envision your ideas through an excited and encouraging lens. The Type 9 is, at core, non-judgmental and seeks to bring harmony to the garden and planet. She is able to sit square in the center of the Enneagram proverbial garden fence, and will seek to find common ground and fertile soil for your chosen flower varieties and placements. And if a garden tussle erupts due to dif-fering preferences for bearded vs. Japanese iris—the 9 Flower Gardener will mediate with a calm and reassuring presence.

In the end, she wants *you and all* to be happy, so she might just live with either choice, even though she isn't a fan of irises. Harmony is the end-game for the 9 Gardener, and she will head down the garden path that resonates tranquility. You see, it is just easier for the Nine to *go-with-the-flow* than to *rock the boat*.

Unfortunately, deep down, under several layers of harmonious mulch, the Type 9 may feel a little bit miffed at once again passing up what she really wants in the garden for the sake of keeping the peace. In the end, just don't give a 9 Flower Gardener too many choices, or you'll end up in a garden game you'll wish you never entered. The Nine is much, much better at voicing her, *I-don't-wants* than her *I-do-wants*—so you can be in for a very long garden party if you start down the path full of 9 Flower Gardener weeds.

# THE WEEDS: THE CHALLENGES
## FOR THE TYPE 9 GARDENER

### FORGET-ME-NINES

The forget-me-not, *Myosotis sylvatica*, is a beautiful, blue woodland flower; however, in this section, I would like to introduce you to the forget-me-Nine! As you read in the Triad section, the instinctual Types "self-forget" in some way or another, and the 9 Flower Gardener does it by forgetting her own self-interests and desires. A somewhat familiar garden dilemma plays out daily: there are just so many *possible* garden tasks and angles to explore, that the Type 9 settles into a cozy garden corner for a nap. But first she'll post a sign on the fence, "Garden in Progress."

Let's just say that the Nine holds a long view of the garden (very, very long!). While the 3 Flower Gardener will have two new gardens developed in a week, and two others in progress, the 9 Gardener may take several months or years to fully realize her garden. She gets a wee-bit distracted by her own myriad life-projects, as well as those of friends and family!

So, on any given day, you might find one of our forget-me-Nines sitting in her hammock, doodling sketches of another friend's garden or starting a pottery mosaic on an old flower pot. In the meantime, the Type 9's garden might be an increasingly neglected tangle of vines, held up by rubber bands and hair ties! The conundrum for the Type 9 is that the multitude of prospects and related decisions for her own garden take far too much energy and time. She then thinks to herself, what's the garden-rush? It's almost September, so why not just put the garden to bed for the winter!

## THE PASSIVE-AGGRESSIVE PLANTER

While most gardeners deer-proof their garden, the 9 Gardener conflict-proofs her garden! She wants nothing more than a peaceful existence, with as few brambles and pests as possible, and she will go to great lengths to keep that peace. In an effort to avoid a tense situation, the Type 9 will almost always take a side path—otherwise called the passive-aggressive route—to obtain resolution.

I have a friend, a 9 Flower Gardener, who was in dispute with her neighbor regarding the neighbor's dog that was unfortunately having his daily constitutional in her flower garden. Seriously, daily poops and an AWOL pooper-scooper! So, my friend went to her neighbor (feeling sure said neighbor had *no idea*) and politely shared the poop-problem. Not only did the neighbor already know, he chuckled about how lucky he was that his dog didn't poop in *his own* flower beds! I. Am. Not. Joking! It takes all kinds to fill a planet!

Well, this scenario, for a Type 9 Gardener, is akin to the mafia running a drug ring in your basement and burying bodies in your petunia bed. While my friend was outraged, she also didn't want to create a scene. So, what did she do?

She just happened to share her situation with another neighbor, who *just happened* to be a One Flower Gardener, who was appalled! Of course, true to Type, the One promptly placed a copy of the *Community Rules, Regulations, and Fines* document in the offending dog-owner's door, with a note to view the "Pet Rules" section. *Voilá*, an electric fence was installed within the week. My 9 Flower Gardener won't forget she was slighted—but instead of outwardly expressing her frustration or anger, she put a pile of mulch on the anger; which will unfortunately pop up like an unwanted weed at another location/time.

## The Meandering Vine

After a fierce thunderstorm, a large, old oak tree uproots and falls across a gardener's back yard. If you ask different Enneagram Flower Gardeners the following question—When did that huge tree fall across your yard?—you'll likely get a variety of responses, true to each Type.

A straightforward Type 8 might respond with an up-front, "Three days ago. I figure it was probably hit by lightning during that bad storm."

The efficient Three might respond: "Arrrgh! A few days ago! That tree provided shade for two of my perennial beds! Probably the trunk will provide a good three seasons of mulch—and I already started ordering plants that will take partial sun because the full-shade perennials won't make it through next summer without the shade."

And then there is the 9 Flower Gardener. My advice is to pull up a chair and pour yourself a tall glass of iced tea, because a Nine will hardly ever, perhaps never, tell a short story. Ask a seemingly simple question such as the above, and the 9 Gardener will launch in to share quite the tale of "the impending storm, and the winds, and my dog had to be calmed due to the lightning, and the cable went out for two hours, during which time I heard a clap of thunder that very well may have struck the oak tree. However, I'm not sure, because I thought that perhaps that tree was dropping leaves the season prior to this one. In fact, I'm wondering if I need a soil test. Speaking of soil tests . . ." and on it goes. You see, the Nine's style of communication is akin to a saga, not a story, so you best settle in and count clover—because you will be listening for a while.

*Nature does not hurry,*
*yet everything is accomplished.*
Lao Tzu

## Knowing When the Type 9 Is in the Brambles (Turn Back!)

When the 9 Flower Gardener finds herself worrying about her garden and becoming overcommitted and anxious, she needs to check that she didn't take the path in the direction of the arrow to the un-resourceful side of the Type 6 garden. In this 9/6 duo, the Nine will begin to doubt her garden plans, which leads to even more indecision. That just won't do, as the generally slow-thinking 9 Gardener becomes a bit "testy" and over-reacts. Even the droopiest of sunflowers will raise their heavy heads to take note.

Instead, I encourage the Type 9 to venture to the *other* side of the Type 6 flower garden, where she will recognize the value of seeing the realistic, up- and down-sides of the garden! She will find her voice and exert her gut opinions with her Type 6 neighbors, to build a peaceful, harmonious, and inclusive community garden.

## How to Find Your Path "Home"

To witness a 9 Flower Gardener flourishing like a mid-spring garden is a wonder to behold! On this path, against the direction of the arrow, the Type 9 chooses to borrow characteristics from the ambitious 3 Flower Gardener and becomes a garden star! In the 9/3 garden space, the indecisive Nine becomes goal-driven and self-confident—in command of her life and flower beds! She can not only find true peace (no feelings of doubt or wasted time and energy) but can truly listen to her instincts and rely on herself and others to move into action. If I could choose a garden to dwell in, I might have to go with this 9/3 merger. Type 9 Peace + Type 3 Productivity = Perfection. Count me in.

> *It's time for you to move, realizing that*
> *the thing you are seeking is also seeking you.*
> Iyanla Vanzant

## THE MEANING OF THE WINDFLOWER

The windflower, anemone, is a beautiful woodland flower that most commonly symbolizes protection against ill will and evil. The translation of the word from Greek mythology means "daughter of the wind" and revolves around the death of Adonis, lover of Aphrodite.

If the windflower is not bold enough for you, consider these other Nine Flower Gardener favorites (also see the Appendix):

**Joe Pye Weed**: To be late or delayed—and Type 9s struggle with time.

**Allium**: Symbolizes patience, humility, and unity.

**Peony**: There when you need them—waiting for you.

**Cosmos**: Pure peace in a flower—that's all.

> *There is no harm in putting off a piece of work until another day.*
> *But when it is a matter of baobabs, that always means a catastrophe.*
> Antoine de Saint-Exupéry, *The Little Prince*

## IN ESSENCE: HORNBEAM FLOWER

"What in the heck is essence of hornbeam flower?" you ask. Well, judge not, my friend—as I'll wager that a good portion of the planet might do with a sniff of hornbeam. In particular, the Type 9 in life and garden can feel that she hasn't sufficient strength, mentally or physically, to carry the burden of the many "to do's" placed upon her; the affairs of every day seem too much for her to accomplish. And though Type 9s generally succeed in fulfilling their tasks, a whiff of hornbeam might be just the ticket! So, for all of you who believe that some part of the mind or body needs to be strengthened before easily fulfilling life's work, an essence is merely a whiff away. Move over, cuppa joe, pour yourself a cup of hornbeam *au lait* with a sprinkle of chocolate!

DISTINCT HUES OF THE
NINE FLOWER GARDENER

*Peaceful*
*Diplomatic*
*Receptive*
*Down To earth*
*Settled*

**Tips for the Type Nine Gardener**

- Stay on one garden task. Finish that task before starting another.
- Recognize your garden zone-out strategies, and try to avoid them.
- You have an opinion about what to plant and where to plant it. Share it.
- Garden frustration is healthy—just don't deadhead when you are angry.
- Your spring garden is calling you; please respond before winter.
- Avoid flower-paralysis and seek out a consultant if you need a garden-hand.
- Be the director of your own garden bed; don't allow others to make it for you.
- Take the direct garden trail. The passive-aggressive route is a dead end.

## The Official Enneagram-in-the-Garden Path Ends Here

But your Enneagram journey is just beginning. Whether through the tear-like buds of the bleeding heart or bearing witness to the purity of a spring calla lily, I hope that you continue to discover the wonders of your garden. As I close, I want to thank the beautiful personalities that grace my world—family members, teachers, and friends who embody the nine Enneagram Types and continue to mentor me with grace and love.

With that, I will turn from these pages and return to my garden, hoping I have left you pondering and perhaps thirsty for a deeper knowledge of the Enneagram to feed your heart, mind, and body. Besides, I have work to do! I'm a Two Flower Gardener, after all.

NOW I SEE THE SECRET
OF MAKING THE BEST PERSON,
IT IS TO GROW IN THE OPEN AIR AND
TO EAT AND SLEEP WITH THE EARTH.

WALT WHITMAN

# Table 1

## Enneagram Flower Gardener Types, Passions, and Tools

| Type Attribute | Passion/ Symbol | Garden Characteristics | Garden Priority Is to ... | Must Have |
|---|---|---|---|---|
| 1 Perfection | Anger/Wasp | Small footprint | Create the perfect row | Hoe |
| 2 Helper | Pride/Ant | Year-round blooms | Nourish the blossoms | Fertilizer |
| 3 Efficient | Deceit/Vole | Show-worthy | Accomplish every task | Multi-purpose tool |
| 4 Aesthetic | Envy/Moth | Rare species | Create unique shapes | Pruning shears |
| 5 Observant | Avarice/ Squirrel | Private spaces | Gather all the leaves | Rake |
| 6 Cautious | Fear/Rabbit | Gate with lock | Weed out invasives | Sunscreen and protective clothing |
| 7 Adventurous | Gluttony/ Deer | More plants | Trellis wandering vines | Garden twine |
| 8 Self-reliant | Lust/ Grasshopper | Hardy plants | Dig a big, ol' hole | Bulldozer |
| 9 Peaceful | Sloth/Slug | Peaceful haven | Nurture the seedlings | Garden gloves |

# TABLE 2

## TYPE PASSION AND DESCRIPTION

| Type | Passion | Description |
|---|---|---|
| **One** <br> **I Am Angry** <br> **But I can't publicly show it** | | I've got some rather rough news for all of you One Gardeners: gardens are rarely, if almost never-ever, *perfect*. For some 1s this is good news because 1's just love a challenge. The bad news is, you might throw in the proverbial garden towel when the aphids get your roses and the snails devour your hosta leaves. We know you are **angry**, behind that forced, sunny smile. Please don't kick the cat or yell at the kids! Remember the *great* is the enemy of the *good*. Gardens are not black (so gorgeous) or white (dig it all up) but many hues! You and your garden are a work in progress so let your frustrations go and smell those roses! |
| **Two** <br> **I Am Proud** <br> **I'm so good to you, and you best crow about it** | | Sorry, Two Gardeners, this may be tough to swallow: you can't ever (never-ever) perceive and meet everyone's needs. You best learn to fertilize your own garden before tending to the world's gardens. For some 2s this is good news, because, they are *plum tuckered out*. The bad news, unfortunately, is that many Two Gardeners are too darn **proud** to realize it until they are limping their way down the garden path with twigs in their hair and sun*burnt to a crisp*. Please take a break before it's too late. You must remember to cradle your own needs in those helpful hands. We promise to love you and your garden, even more if you do. |
| **Three** <br> **I Am Deceptive** <br> **I must act my roles, and I don't even know it** | | Imagine a movie scene, *In the Garden of Good and Evil*—the garden is your stage and you are the star actor, dazzling the audience with a vast array of blossoms and tiered garden beds. CUT! CUT! Take II! Or better yet, *wake up*. The Type 3 Gardener is literally living a dream, or in this case, enacting a movie. In reality, the Three is **deceiving** herself, and others, by believing she is the star in a myriad of plays. If the 3 Gardener could only stop, put down the Oscar, and realize that being herself, in her own, true-life role—with (at times) a moderately productive garden and supporting role—will always deliver her best performance. |

TABLE 2

## TYPE PASSION AND DESCRIPTION

| Four | |
|---|---|
| **I Am Envious** | Fours, please stop peeing over that fence right now, or you and the whole trellis may come tumbling down! Put the ladder away and pull up a rocking chair to sit a spell in your own backyard. For Type 4s, the issue is seeing "green," and I'm not talk'n leaves. You see, 4 Gardeners are green with **envy**. It seems to the 4 that everyone has it a bit better than they do—be it a better garden or a better life, in general. This comes from a place that is well-deep, and when they draw up the water they can't see their own reflection—only that of the "other" that they long to find. If only, with grace and wisdom, they could see that their own reflection *is* perfection. |
| **I must find what is missing and what I lack below it** | |

| Five | |
|---|---|
| **I Am Avaricious** | Is life in the garden really that demanding? To the Type 5, the answer is a full stop YES. Type 5 Gardeners in the garden and life prefer to keep themselves on the "low down"—as in perhaps *underground!* The Type 5 is akin to a garden squirrel burying nuts in a geranium pot, except the Five is **avariciously** hoarding goods and information, guarding what she has and knows. This is an effort to feel "full" and avoid the emptiness she feels inside, basically keeping her "goods" and detaching from the fuss and the noise. |
| **I must conserve my energy and act like I know it (all)** | |

| Six | |
|---|---|
| **I Am Fearful** | While most would say their garden is about as far away from a "disaster zone" as any place on the earth—this is regretfully not true for the 6 Gardener. **Fear** is the bane of the Type 6, and their fear puts them out of touch with their inner self-confidence and reality. Unfortunately, this drives the Type 6 into seeing garden peril in every flower bed. This creates a conundrum, as the Six must be prepared to counter the myriad of things (aphids and June bugs and snails—Oh my!) that could be out to get her and her defenseless, fragile-flower buds. The 6 Flower Gardener might even suspect *you!* |
| **Of what may be coming—and I don't yet know it** | |

TABLE 2

TYPE PASSION AND DESCRIPTION

| | |
|---|---|
| **Seven** | |
| **I Am Gluttonous** | Don't be a stick in the mud: join the 7 Gardener in overindulging in life and the garden! Because the Type 7 has a teensy-weensy problem with the concept of *everything in moderation*, their passion is **gluttony**, referring to excesses in future-tripping, excitement, stuff, events. Hmmm. Did I say, "everything from seeds to sod"? I did. The Seven just |
| **I must have positivity and grow it** | doesn't know when to quit. Why all of this "more"? To appear happy and mask the sadness—the Type 7 just can't tolerate the weight of problems, so she fills her basket with a weightless bouquet of joy. |
| **Eight** | |
| **I Am Lustful** | The 8 Gardener is always ready for a good ol' garden brawl! Bring on the mud-slinging and the 8 will be at the ready to defend her turf. Type 8s wake up every single day expecting trouble or perhaps someone ready to take advantage of them or their petal pals. Basically, the Eight needs to "get there" first—so she goes forward with gusto and |
| **I must be strong and not blow it** | can become a bit grabby and demanding. Excess and **lust** are the names of the game for the Type 8 Gardeners, so you best be on your game if you ante up! Otherwise, call in your mulch chips and head home. |
| **Nine** | |
| **I Am Slothful** | A garden is full of choices—and like many spheres of life, the 9 Gardener experiences self-doubt and indecision when exploring her options. The end result is procrastination, confusion, and inaction—all leading to a nap in the hammock! Or perhaps a distraction elsewhere? The Nine will find something else to occupy her time and energy, especially |
| **I can't rock the boat—I'd rather flow in the boat than row it** | when it comes to tackling anything disturbing or laden with conflict. In times of high stress, the Type 9 takes the first flight to Costa Rica and communes with her treasured **Sloth**. *Pura Vida!* |

# TABLE 3: FLOWER, SCIENTIFIC NAME, REASON, PREFERENCE

## Type 1

| Rose | *Rosa* | Because, like the Type 1, the rose is just perfect. | Sun |
| Coneflower | *Echinacea* | Known for its native medicinal qualities and a seed provider for birds. | Sun |
| Butterfly Weed | *Asclepias tuberosa* | Attracts hummingbirds and hordes of butterflies, bees, and other beneficial insects. | Sun |
| Goldenrod | *Solidago* | Amazing health benefits, including reduction of pain and inflammation. | Sun |
| Sunflower | *Helianthus* | In areas where soil pollution is high, plants such as sunflowers may be grown in order to help clean up the environment. | Sun |

## Type 2

| Zinnia | *Zinnia* | A true-2 flower, meaning thoughts of friends, remembrance, and lasting affection. | Sun |
| Geranium | *Pelargonium* | Symbolizes true friendship and is super comforting. | Sun |
| Coreopsis (Tickseed) | *Coreopsis* | Just as cheerful as can be. | Sun |
| Butterfly Bush | *Buddleia davidii* | Provides a loving home for yellow swallowtail butterflies | Sun |
| Forget-Me-Not | *Myosotis* | Every Type 2's request—just don't forget them. | Sun |

# TABLE 3: FLOWER, SCIENTIFIC NAME, REASON, PREFERENCE

## Type 3

| Flower | Scientific Name | Reason | Preference |
|---|---|---|---|
| Hollyhock | *Alcea rosea* | So darn ambitious—just keeps on blooming when the heat is on. | Sun |
| Bear's Breeches | *Acanthus Mollis* | Represents artifice, so best be aware of the nemesis in the garden. | Pt. Sun |
| Daphne | *Daphne Odora* | Ah, Fame and Glory to the Daphne! | Pt. Sun |
| Hydrangea | *Hydrangea macrophylla* | You're so vain . . . you probably think this flower's about ya'! | Pt. Sun |
| Phlox | *Phlox* | Means "flame" and attracts showy butterflies. | Pt. Sun Shade |

## Type 4

| Flower | Scientific Name | Reason | Preference |
|---|---|---|---|
| Orchid | *Orchidaceae* | So elegant—and makes a long-lasting impression on us all. | Pt. Sun Shade |
| Sweet William | *Dianthus barbatus* | The name means "Grant Me One Smile." | Sun |
| Columbine | *Aquilegia* | Unique and reminds us of deserted love. | Pt. Shade |
| Bleeding Heart | *Lamprocapnos* | What a perfect Type 4 name, right? And it means to love unconditionally with an open heart. | Pt. Sun |
| Fuchsia | *Fuchsia* | Over 100 species in the evening primrose family—simply stunning. | Pt. Sun Shade |

## TABLE 3: FLOWER, SCIENTIFIC NAME, REASON, PREFERENCE

### Type 5

| | | | |
|---|---|---|---|
| Bloodroot | *Sanguinaria* | Protective love and healing. | Shade |
| Cactus | *Cactaceae* | As calm as can be. | Sun |
| Sea Holly | *Eryngium* | Because this plant is just fine when left alone. | Sun Pt. Shade |
| Salvia (Sage) | *Salvia officinalis* | Oh so wise—and the scent makes me feel smart. | Sun |
| Hearts-a-Bustin' | *Euonymous americanus* | Named for the plant's unique four-lobed capsules that "bust" open to reveal bright-red seed hearts. | Shade |

### Type 6

| | | | |
|---|---|---|---|
| Lavender | *Lavendula* | Loyalty and calm in a flower and an essential oil. | Sun |
| Begonia | *Begonia* | Be cautious and think deeply. | Shade Pt. Sun |
| Datura | *Datura* | Poison! Sometimes known as the Devil's Trumpet. Spooky, huh? | Sun |
| Spiderwort | *Tradescantia* | Named after its spidery sap, symbolizes moral authority. And let's face it, every Type 6 expects to find a big ol' spider in the garden. | Pt. Shade |
| Iris | *Iris germanica* | Because ya' gotta' have faith. | Sun Pt. Shade |

## TABLE 3: FLOWER, SCIENTIFIC NAME, REASON, PREFERENCE

### Type 7

| | | | |
|---|---|---|---|
| Clematis | *Clematis* | Because it wants to be everywhere and has lots of tendrils. | Sun |
| Poppy | *Papaver* | Imagination, oblivion, and pleasure. | Sun |
| Marigold | *Tagetes* | Because they are happy as can be. | Sun |
| Chrysan-themum | *Chrysanthemum morifolium* | Excitement and optimism. | Sun |
| Calendula | *Calendula officinalis* | Folk name is "summer's bride," as the flower head turns as the summer sun moves through the sky. | Sun |

### Type 8

| | | | |
|---|---|---|---|
| Black-eyed Susan | *Rudbeckia hirta* | They are just downright bold, and there's no hiding them. | Sun |
| Camellia | *Camellia* | Strong desire and excellence, even when it's really cold outside. | Pt. Shade |
| Foxglove | *Digitalis* | Means insincerity, and Type 8s know it when they see it. | Sun Pt. Shade |
| Gladiolus | *Gladiolus* | They stand tall and are known for their strength of character. | Sun |
| Angel's Trumpet | *Brugmansia* | Signifies vivacity, health, and also danger. | Sun |

## TABLE 3: FLOWER, SCIENTIFIC NAME, REASON, PREFERENCE

### Type 9

| | | | |
|---|---|---|---|
| Windflower | *Anemonastrum* | Peaceful like a gentle breeze. | Pt. Shade |
| Joe Pye Weed | *Eutrochium perpureum* | To be late or delayed—9s struggle with this one. | Pt. Sun Shade |
| Allium | *Allium* | Symbolizes patience, humility, and unity. | Sun |
| Peony | *Paeonia* | There when you need them, waiting for you. | Sun |
| Cosmos | *Cosmos bipinnatus* | Pure peace in a flower—that's it. | Sun |

ACKNOWLEDGMENTS

Over the past twenty-five years, a great many people have graced my garden journey. I cannot possibly thank all of them—but it is important to be grateful for my garden-mentors. A year ago, when I began writing this book in earnest, I didn't tell a soul because, quite frankly, I never thought I'd complete it. Now looking back, how could I not? When I finally tentatively shared my early ideas and writing with a few dear friends they cheered me along, eagerly asking about my progress—Deb, Donna, Kathleen, Milley, Dawn, Kristine, Lynn—thank you for encouraging me. I am so very appreciative for the many women in my life; I am so much richer for their insights and support. I am deeply beholden to a small group advance readers for their time and expertise. Thank you so very much for your supportive and constructive feedback.

For my editor and champion—Mary Neighbour—so grateful I am. You see, while I'm not one to suggest a certain Enneagram type is better for a particular avocation, I must admit I was secretly thrilled when we determined Mary is a Type Five. Her thorough and thoughtful editing process, wise suggestions, and calm re-assurances have been my rock during this process. This book would not be in your hands without Mary by my side.

When I began writing this book, I had a vague idea about the types of images that might be included, but I honestly wasn't sure of what was possible. Hui Jing Ng swiftly took care of that after I saw my initial "ideas" take shape and color in her talented hands. I dare say that she has proved herself as an Enneagram illustrator *extraordinaire*. Over the last eight months, I have eagerly opened my inbox each day to see her images that, at times, took my breath away. I cannot thank her enough for bringing the images *in my head* to life.

To my sister JoAnn, who introduced me to the Enneagram so many years ago, and has always supported my ideas and initiatives—no matter what. I am so thankful for her unconditional love and support. And finally, to my husband, Marty, who listened to my doubts (did I say, daily?), encouraged me every step of the writing process, read every single draft, and read them again. I thank you with all of my heart. This book is dedicated to you.

# About the Author

Dr. Angela Rosenberg, DrPH, focuses on leadership development and advancement of individuals and teams, through her company, Inside Out. She is a Board Certified Leadership Coach (BCC) who uses a variety of assessment approaches in her workshops and retreats; the Enneagram is, admittedly, her favorite. She has presented and consulted on team-building approaches and strategic planning with numerous national organizations and has authored publications in several peer-reviewed journals.

Angela also wrote and illustrated *The Shell and Me*, a children's book. She gardens on her North Carolina farm where she lives with her husband, Great Danes, a Golden Doodle, donkeys, and one brave cat. *Nine Perfect Petals: The Enneagram for Flower Gardeners* is her first book for adults and Book 1 in the Enneagram in Nature Series.

Printed in the USA
CPSIA information can be obtained
at www.ICGtesting.com
LVHW071927031023
760019LV00018B/558

9 781736 676721